A MEMOIR OF
THE RAPIER'S

Copyright © 2020 by Arlene Janoski.

ISBN-978-1-6485-8112-0

All rights reserved. No part of this book may be reproduced or transmitted in any form or by any means, electronic or mechanical, including photocopying, recording, or by any information storage and retrieval system, without permission in writing from the copyright owner.

The views expressed in this work are solely those of the author and do not necessarily reflect the views of the publisher, and the publisher hereby disclaims any responsibility for them.

Matchstick Literary
1-888-306-8885
orders@matchliterary.com

A MEMOIR OF THE RAPIER'S

Life and History

Arlene Janoski

Dedicated to our parents:
Clarence Thomas Rapier
May 13, 1899-January 9, 1979
Elsie Mae Shaw Rapier
April 2, 1903-June 12, 1986

Stories told at our family gatherings were interesting, fascinating, and amazing. Before these stories vanish from memory, I feel the need to set them down for the generations to come.

Interwoven here are family traditions, Homespun yarns, facts, and history of our family. These ordinary people lived the trying days of wars, illness, the loss of loved ones, and the Great Depression. Nevertheless, they endured to the end.

"---let us run with patience the race that is set before us—
Apostle Paul in Hebrews Chapter 12 Verse 1
King James Bible

CONTENTS

1. England 1
2. America 5
3. William and Rutha Raper 9
4. Larkin Webb Raper 11
5. Jacob Asbury Raper/Rapier 28
6. Clarence Thomas (Tommy) Rapier 34
7. Elsie Mae Shaw 61
8. Sod Busters 77
9. The Journey 92

1

ENGLAND

The name Raper is rooted in the ancient Anglo-Saxon culture and is found in medieval documents. It seems to derive from the trade of rope making or sailing. The Old English word for rope was RAP. There are many spellings for RAPER, i.e., Roper, Rooper, and Rapier. Spelling depended mainly on the pronunciation pretty much as the writer wished, of course, until the English Dictionary was compiled. My immediate family preferred Rapier.

A Rodger Raper is recorded in the records of Yorkshire as early as 1219.

One member of the Raper family was the original instigator in mapping out plans for the round-the-world trip with a fleet of ships, which later was carried out by Magellan. This Raper refused the leadership of that historic voyage, due to a disagreement and falling out with the Government of England.

Francis Hawkins and Drake made their first slave-trading voyage to America in 1562, and between 1563 and 1564, finally, peace was negotiated between England and France

Following the crusades in Europe a need was felt for a family name to replace one given at birth, or in addition to it. This name was then recognized by those of noble birth and particularly by those who went on the crusades, as it added prestige and practical advantage to their status.

Decades of religious tension followed the break from the Church by King Henry VIII. This break kicked off persecution for those practicing the Catholic faith.

The world was full of turmoil. Nevertheless; there were a few significant historical events. As in 1552, the Duke of Somerset was executed. The much awaited son, Edward, of Henry VIII and Jane Seymour was born. However, he was a weak child and a disappointment to his father. Edward developed tuberculosis,. In 1553, the Duke of Northumberland persuaded the then fifteen year old Edward to proclaim Lady Jane Grey, the 16 years old, as his heir in an attempt to secure Protestant succession. However, when Edward dies Lady Jane became the Queen of England. Her reign lated only nine days.

Mary, the daughter of Henry VIII and Catherine of Aragon was not happy as she was a devout Catholic and overtakes the throne. Therefore Lady Jane Grey was arrested which made the Protestants in the land very angry and they revolted.

This revolt further angeried Mary and had manyProtestants burned for heresy. Mary also repealed Ptrotestant legislation and restored England to Catholicism and Papal supremacy. The cruelties perpetuated resulted in Mary's nickname "BLOODY MARY." Soon Lady Jane Grey and her husband were both executed.

In 1555 three Protestants and bishops were burned at the stake for hersey. In 1556, Thomas Crammer, former Archbishop of Canterbury was also burned at the stake.

Enland declared was on France in 1557 and Mary died in 1558.

Elizabeth, the Virgin Queen, assumes the throne and defies the mostly Catholic Europe. Under Elizabeth's reign and her political skill there was a vast expantion in English trade. However, under Elizabeth's reign approximately 50,000 English women were accused of being witches and excuted.

In 1570 the Pope excommunicated Queen Elizabeth from the Church.

During his reign, King James did not grant toleration of Catholics and failed to end the persecution. Conspirators hoped to kill the King and install a ruler friendlier to Catholics. So, planning to blow up the House of Lords when King James came for the opening of Parliament a tunnel was dug under the House of Lords and filled the area with barrels of gunpowder. Guy Fawkes, one of the conspirators, who was on guard in the tunnel when the plot was foiled.

n 1606, a law was passed against the Roman Catholics. At this period, of time, William Shakespeare wrote King Lear and these who quotes from King Lear that apply eflect the era: "Who is it that can tell me who I am?"

and "The weight of this sad time we must obey." King James wanting to appease the Puritans and authorized the King James Bible in 1611. King James could not have cared less about the Bible itself. It was shocking to many that a gay King, as a political move, authorized the Bible.

In 1585, Marmaduke Bowes was charged with the crime of concealing Catholic Priests in his home and hanged. He most likely hid the priests to educate his children. His sons, Robert and Thomas, sold half the grange, in the Parish of Welbury, Yorkshire, to Edward Raper in 1607. When Edward died in 1620, his son, George, inherited his father's holdings.

Two disasters struck London during the 1660's. Fleas carried the bubonic plague, in which more than 75,000 people died. A fire started in a bakery near London Bridge destroyed most of the city including 13,000 houses, St. Paul's Cathedral, 84 churches, markets, wharves. Buildings were blown up to make gaps so the fire could not cross the Thames River. The conflagration continued to rage four days.

An inscription is on a chalice of one Tho: Gregory William Raper, a Church warden at Topcliffe Church, Yorkshire dated March 26, 1664.

There are many Raper's mentioned in wills and letters. There also are Raper's who studied at Cambridge during the 17th Century.

Coat of Arms was awarded by the College of Heralds to knights and dames, to nobles, or the companies that have achieved a certain status. During the sixteenth century the RAPER family acquired the Coat of Arms with Crest from the government of England. This was a distinguishing mark by which a family might be identified and signifying the Mark of Honor.

"To these Ensignes of Honor, as commonly called Armes, which of later times have been chiefly used for distinctions of families, had their origin from the practice of great commanders in War, is not unknown to the learned, for certain it is, that the faces of all great military officers, being obscured by such Hoods and Helmets, as were anciently worn in times of Battle, it was expedient, that by some means their persons should be notified to their friends and followers. Necessity, therefore requiring it, they depicted upon their Surcoats and shields, certain badges that make them known at a distance from each other."

The description or Representation of the Coat of Arms of the Raper family, is recorded in the College of Arms and Heralds in London, England. The description is as follows:

> Per Fesse – a shield parted in center by horizontal lines.
> Wavy – the curved line undulating like waves of the sea.
> Az – Azure, French word meaning blue.
> Ar – Agent, French word meaning silver.
> A Pale Counter – changed – 2 perpendicular lines vertical.
> Erased – head of the Antelope.
> Or – French word for Gold.
> Crest – above the shield, highest part of the Coat of Arms, and signifying the mark of honor.
> This Coat of Arms is shared by all RAPER's of Yorkshire, lineage including Matthew of London.

There many Raper's in York, England in the 1600's. Apparently they were gentlemen and men of means.

Matthew Raper, a silk merchant in London, was born in 1653 in London, and lived in the Parish of St. Martin, Ironmonger Lane, later moving to White Lion Court, Cornhill. He was elected to the Court of the Bank of England in 1772.

In 1672 King Charles II issued a declaration granting religious freedom. However, in 1673 Parliament forced Charles II to withdraw that declaration and to pass the Test Act requiring officials to belong to the Church of England, which kept Catholics out of public office. Many Catholicswere persecuted in the ensuing years.

Another Henry Raper has a will written March 24, 1675, and describes himself of Cowl, daughter Cordelia (James Wishart), and another daughter born later was Henrietta, who never married. Another Henry and Thomas Raper owned the Manor in 1706.

2

AMERICA

The American Colonial Army begins to fight for freedom from England.

Resulting that in March 5,1771 there was the Boston Massacre and in 1773- Boston Tea Party.

There was a John Raper, merchant, of South Carolina who gave a Power of Attrony on Febuary 3, 1731, to Robert Raper and James Neale. I have a copy in my files. They apparently first settled in South Carolina, America.

Diets in America were somewhat different than the English. Mostly the American diet consisted of wheat, rice, oats, and beans. There were potatoes, mushrooms, legumes, and onions. Their meat was turkey, quail, and geese. However, Elizabeth Raper shows that the America women had other menus. While the political unrest was ongoing, Elizabeth was only interested in her home life and cooking. The following excerpts are from, "The receipt Book of Elizabeth Raper. The book was written between 1756-1770 and passed down through the family. It contains potion of Elizabeth's personal journal (Diary), giving a wonderful insight into the life and times of an upper-class family in 18th century. She describes the house, grounds, clothing, food, social events – and her admirers and suitors.

The second part of the book contains recipes that Elizabeth collected. Her instructions for cooking various dishes give a glimpse of the 18th-century kitchen. It is a fascinating read. Anthony Raper has transformed the book to CD, which can be printed out directly. If you would like a Copy; please contact him at anthony raper@btopenworld.com. (3)

Miss Raper was a noted housekeeper and cook, and these recipes testify to her practical knowledge of cookery. Her brothers persistently objected to her marrying any of those she inclined to, announced that 'if she could not marry to please herself, she would not marry to please them. She leans backward in giving them encouragement."

Excerpts from Elizabeth's journal:
"In Mrs. How's dressing room blundered on some discourse? I know not how, which gave me the Terrys. Wish to God I could bury in oblivion all that passed 5 years ago, but alas! It's still fresh in my memory, fool that I am, but if it must remain, let it be for a hint, thou a cursed bad one, in regard to mankind."

"Up, Biki. Had scarce done when Mr. Hotham came, but could not stay he said, routed out a Bass and played to us, well Then he staid to dinner, but was to go before dark, then it misled, then it grew darkish, then wrote and sent him instead of going, soon very facetious, pretty good friends, romped, but not all that, supped, had a long argument, he and I, concerning matrimony, managing wives, what degree of learning a woman ought to have, etc, etc, liked my conversation very well and believe he did not dislike it, both agreed, though both differed. Not in bed till one. N. B. Miss Cleeve and I dressed up a Joan and put it in his bed."

Baft. Over we all walked in the garden, the lover very pensive, kept close to me, sighed, squeezed and sighed again, his mother looked very arch but said not a word."

Recipes:

TO TURTLE A CALF'S HEAD

The Calf's head must be scalded and not flead, cut in slices about the size of a crown piece. Take also some neats foot, stew these in good veal broth, put it an onion, a faggot of sweet herbs, half a pint of Madeira (or any white wine that is not sweet) and a teaspoonful of red pepper, keep it stewing til quite tender, and serve it up in your Tureen with forced mat ball, and yolks of eggs boiled hard.

A PLAIN PLUMB CAKE

2 pound of flour, 6 ounces of butter, 5 ounces of sugar, a pound and quarter of currants, some spice, a little salt, 5 or 6 spoonfuls of yeast, mix with warm milk, this makes three cakes. You may bake them in tin pans.

A FLOUR PUDDEN

A pint of milk, 5 eggs, 3 spoonfuls of flour worked up all together, (the milk first boiled with cinnamon and Bay leaves and put to cool to it) a little salt, boiled in a bason (basin) for ¾ of an hour, sugar, butter, and wine for the sauce.

In the back of the book, there are a few additional recipes not written by Elizabeth's hand. Most seem to be medicinal. I liked this one.

A PURGING PITISAN

Take eight blanched sweet Almonds. One ounce and a half of best flake Manna, half an ounce of soluble tartar. Beat them well together in a Mortar and then add by degrees two Gills of the simple Cinnamon Water. Strain this mixture and take a teacup full every hour till it operates.

http://www.codepot.net/raper/4641020653859.html   7/11/2002

The Stream called Abbotts Creek

There is a story about Abbotts Creek that when Lord Cornwallis tried to go on Crofts Bridge across the creek he was carrying a barrel of gold and silver coin and did not make it. Apparently the the barrel is buried in the depths of the creek and from that day ghosts have haunted the vincinity. Ghosts frieghten horse back riders. Also strange light are seen at night, and the barrel of coin is heard to roll around. Hunters are lost and dogs are unable to tree the possum. Many such legions are taken seriously in this area.

'For more than a century and a half, the name of William Raper has been associated with the section known as the Abbotts Creek Community. The Raper family was closely associated wth the Shiloh Church, Camden County, This church was the oldest Baptist Church in North Carolina, established in 1727.

In 1817, we find in the records that 'Our Deacon' William Raper is appointed as 'our trustee' to receive contributions, and to correspond with such missionary as may be appointed for the Sandy Creek Association. Thus early begins the intimate association of the name Raper and Abbotts Creek, which continues to this day.

This is how distance measured at this time: ---extended for one-quarter mile in every directin from the "black Oak" that marked the junction of the stagecoach routes that junctioned there at the black oak from Salem to Fayettesville, and Salisbury to Deep River.

The Raper family was apparently very involved in their church.

Notice that in a Petition to Tennessee State Legislature – Monroe- 1820 t0 18.

(14-183) From Bradley, McMinn, Monroe to form new county (Polk (62-1842) to abolish slavery.

(60-184) 6th brigade militia composed of Roane, McMinn, Polk and Bradley including 10 regiments---ask repeal of law to abolish spring muster.

The King Chiefs of Warriors of the Chickasaw Nation was involved in local affairs. See petition of 5-1821-1.

3

WILLIAM AND RUTHA RAPER GREAT-GREAT GRANDPARENTS

In some documents F's and P's appeared to be S's. Therefore Raper seems to be Raser

William Raber was born in 1795, the same year his father William, died. At 19, William joined the Tennessee Calvary Military under Captain Matthew Young and served in the War of 1812 and was discharged in September 1815. He married Rutha when he was about 20, and she was 16. They had 9 children: Elizabeth, John Stafford, Sarah Dye, Meredith, Larkin Webb, Mary Mahala, James Harrison Riley, and Martha. What is the name of the ninth child????s. William died November 26, 1839 in Cleveland, Tennessee

There is a small road at the edge of Madisonville called 'Raper Road.' It is unknown which Raper this road was named for. Rutha Hicks (Raper) the daughter of Shadrack Hicks, and Elizabeth (Nash) was born in 1799 and lived 48 years longer than her husband Rutha die July 1, 1887. Shadrack Hicks the son of John and Comfort (Malone) Hicks was born in 1775. Shadrack was living in Virginia, one of the 13 colonies, in 1776 when Thomas Paine's Common Sense was published and the Declaration of Independence was written.

Rutha evidently did not get action concerning her petition for a Widow's Pension until 1879.

Shadrack married Elizabeth Nash, and had one child, my great-great-grandmother Rutha Jane. He moved to Sullivan County, Tennessee and later to McMinn County. At age 71 Shadrack died in July 1846.

4

LARKIN WEBB RAPER

A GREAT-GRANDFATHER

History has recorded that in the Civil War or War of the Rebellion, there were more battles fought in Tennessee, during the Civil War than in all the other states, except Virginia.

From the Southern point of view, this was a War of Rebellion, a war of Southern Independence. The Northern point of view was a revolution.

Years of profound economic, social and political differences existed between the Union and Confederacy. Moreover, Abraham Lincoln's election was viewed as a threat to slavery. (9)

The war in Tennessee included half-dozen significant battles, and hundreds of skirmishes, between the army of the Union and the army of the Confederate States of America. Fathers and brothers had left home to fight and thousands of boys 17 years or younger entered military service as drummers, musicians, or soldiers in the ranks. My great-grandfather, Larkin Webb Raper, along with brothers and cousins, left their homes, wives, and children, to fight. Marauding armies, guerrillas, deserters, and some regular soldiers from both armies, traversing the state, harassed civilians and many perished at these men's hands. The very worst of the bushwhackers were young boys between fourteen and eighteen.

"Revenge took many forms, from murder to a dousing a man in honey who guided foragers during the war to his neighbors' corn cribs and beehives."

Organized on October 12, 1861, and reorganized May 8, 1862; formed

Company "G" third Consolidated Tennessee Infantry Regiment April 9, 1865; paroled at Greensboro, North Carolina, May 1, 1865. The regiment was known as the East Tennessee Regiment, for the first two years, it was the 31st.

Co. K- First organization: Henderson Hix, Captain; Moses McLendon, first Lieutenant; Hugh B. Henderson, Second Lieutenant; Wm. J. Woods, Third Lieutenant; Second Lieutenant; John H. Henderson, Third Lieutenant;

Shortly after organization, on April 30, 1862, the regiment moved to Loudon with 363 active men, partly armed with country rifles. Brigadier General S. M. Barton's Brigade was composed of the 20th Alabama and 40th Georgia.

Larkin Raperas in the 39th Tennessee Infantry Regiment. Also included were the 9th Georgia Infantry Battalion, and the Botetourt Artillery. A few days later, on the third of July, it was in Brigadier General C. L. Stevenson's Division, Colonel T. H. Taylor's Brigade, composed of the 3rd, 46th Alabama, 3rd (Vaughn's), 39th, 59th Tennessee Infantry Regiments and the Rhett Artillery. These three Tennessee regiments remained together throughout the war.

On Sep. 18, it set out to join General Braxton Bragg's Army of the Mississippi, reaching him at Harrodsburg, Kentucky, just after the Battle of Perryville and retreated with his army to Knoxville. Company. Reports show they marched from Loudon to Camp Breckinridge, Danville, Harrodsburg, Versailles, Lawrenceburg, Kentucky, back via Bryantsville and Lancaster, Kentucky. They went on to Cumberland Gap, Bean's Station, Rutledge, Knoxville, Lenoir, Louden, Tennessee. This march of 700 miles was accomplished in 42 days. Some soldiers often traveled without food or water. Many of the men were barefoot, sometimes in dust four inches deep, and to cap the climax. October 26th, heavy snow, caught the men with no tents, thin clothing, and no cover.

(10) "Tennessee History" by Wilma Dykeman p. 97.

Walt Whitman, while spending several months visiting and nursing Civil War veterans was deeply moved. His brother was also a wounded Union soldier in Washington D. C. During this time he penned the poem "By the Bivouac's Fitful Flame" that tells the story.

A MEMOIR OF THE RAPIER'S

> By the Bivouac's Fitful Flame,
> A procession winding around me, solemn and
> sweet and slow – but first I note,
> The tents of the sleeping army, the fields and wood's dim outline,
> The darkness by spots of kindled fire, the silence,
> Like a phantom far or near an occasional figure moving,
> The shrubs and trees, (as I lift my eyes they
> seem to be stealthily watching me,)
> While wind in procession there as I sit on the ground,
> By the bivouac's fitful flame.

For both the North and South, the Mississippi River served as a vital waterway for mid-western farmers shipping their goods. Control of the Mississippi River was an economic and psychological factor. For the Confederacy, the power of the lower Mississippi River was vital to the union of its states. The area of Louisiana west of the river plus Texas and Arkansas held manpower and material that the rest of the southern military needed.

Vicksburg was the key as President Lincoln stated. The map of the Mississippi River shows that the river's hairpin turn in front of Vicksburg, which sat high on bluffs above the river, made boats traveling in both directions vulnerable to artillery fire. Confederate batteries sat on the shoreline and on the high terrain.

There were four phases of the Vicksburg campaign.

1. In the spring of 1862 upriver attack by Union gunboats.
2. General U. S. Grant's fall campaign, which involved the invasion of north Mississippi and an attempt to flank the Confederates with General William T. Sherman's Mississippi River expedition to a point just north of Vicksburg called Chickasaw Bayou.
3. General Grant launched his spring 1863 campaign of diversions that eventually allowed him to get his army across the river south of Vicksburg.
4. Grant's hard-hitting overland campaign into central Mississippi and his siege operations at Vicksburg.

During the night of April 30 – May 1, 1863, General Grant crossed his army from Louisiana into Mississippi.

Grant's army tried twice to overwhelm Pemberton's army, and, having failed, settled in for a siege ultimately lasted 47 days.

The Confederate soldiers in the trenches lost weight, became dehydrated, and suffered from severe malnutrition.

(11) Michael B. Ballard, Ph. D. is an archivist in Mississippi State University's Mitchell Memorial Library. He is the author of five books, including A Long Shadow: Jefferson Dais and the Final Days of the Confederacy, and Pemberton: A Biography.

December 31, 1862, the regiment left Charleston via rail for Jackson, Mississippi where it arrived ten days and nights in crowded boxcars. They moved on to Vicksburg, Mississippi, where the regiment was engaged in picket duty for some time. In February 1863, detachments of three companies were on a small steam ferryboat with two cannons captured the Federal gunboat "Queen of the West" the Webb, and the ironclad gunboat the "Indianola." On returning to Vicksburg, the tired men spent 47 days in the rain and mud-filled trenches until the surrender of Vicksburg July 4, 1863. J. B. Colvert, D. B. Curtis, J. F. Strickland, Lieut. G. K. Roberts was wounded. Those who died were S. Lockhart, S. Bell, M. H. Bowers, A. D. Carr, Larken Raper, and J.N. Neal. <u>Larken Webb Raper</u> died April 17, 1863. Larkin's brother, Meredith Henry Raper, served in the same company and survived to live a long full life.

After several years, some company officers in many instances have failed to respond to inquiries for information, and many have forgotten. Therefore, the list of killed, wounded, and dead is imperfect and inaccurate.

At least sixteen Raper men were in the Confederate Army. Likely related by blood were the Raper's, Hicks, and Hammontree's listed.

1. Andrew J. Raper Sgt. K Co. 62 MI
2. Andrew J. Raper Sgt. K Co. 62nd MI
3. Deson I. Raper Pvt. H Co. (Dillard's) MI
4. Dison J. Raper Cpl. K Co. MI
5. H. H. Raper Pvt. K Co. Inf.
6. LarkinW. Raper Pvt K Co. 38th MIj

7. Meredith H. Raper Cpl K Co. 39th Mi8.
8. H. H. Raper Pvt. K Co. Inf.
9. Monroe Raper Cpl K Co. 62nd MI
10. Newton Raper Cpl. K Co. 62nd MI
11. Newton J. Raper Pvt. G Co. 2nd (Ashby's) Cav
12. Newton J. Raper Pvt. B Co. 4th Can. BN
13. P. Raper Pvt. B Co. 29th Inf.
14. Thomas Raper Pvt. K Co. 62nd MI
15. William Raper Pvt. G Co. 62nd MI
16. William T. Raper Pvt. F Co. 59th MI

It is sad that many brave men fell in this war. The total deaths exceeded 600,000, and the dead combined totaled about 1.1 million. It is astonishing to note that more Americans died in the Civil War than in all other American wars combined from the colonial period through the later phase of the Vietnam War.

Larkin who was 35, when he died April 17, 1863, in the rain and mud of Mississippi during the Civil War, could not witness his seventeen-year-old son, Jacob's, marriage to eighteen-year-old Delilah Gorman Long, December 8, 1872. Larkin did not get to know his six beautiful grandchildren: Vesta Nora, George, Lillie, Floyd, William (Willie), and Elmer.

Larkin W. Raper Rank: Private
State Served: Tennessee
Unit: 39th Mounted Infantry Regiment Company: K
Born 15 Feb 1828 Sweetwater, Monroe, Tenn.
Died: 17 April 1863
Burial: Cedar Hill Cemetery Vicksburg,
Warren County, Mississippi, USA
Plot: Soldier's Rest.5
Terresse Ellen Hammontree Raper
A great-grandmother.

Note: How my great-grandmother and her children actually traveled from Tennessee to Missouri is not known.

The Raven Mocker, Kalanu Ahkyeliski, a Harbinger from Hell came in the night. His wings and tail blazed a trail of sparks as a shrill shriek split his beak. *Kalanu Ahkyeliski* entered the house unseen, uninvited, swooped down over Larkin to devour his heart.

RUN! RUN! Terresse screamed. However, the sound did not escape her paralyzed throat. This nightmare had plagued her for a month of sleepless nights.

She rose pulling the sweat-soaked nightgown over her head, wrapping a quilt around her shoulders; stumbling to the fireplace to stir the remaining coals adding a few sticks of wood. Finally, the glow of the fire helped to drive the nightmare away as sunrise splintered through the window curtains.

Terresse uttered a prayer as she rocked, *"The Lord is My Shepherd; I shall not want."* she envisioned Larkin's body lowered into an open grave. *"He maketh me to lie down in green pastures."*

"Is my husband dead: Is it green where his body lay?"

To the Cherokee, the "real people," Kalanu Ahkyeliski, the Raven Mocker, is the most dreaded of all the witches. The four souls of the victim of Kalanu Ahkyeliski, reside in his saliva, blood, bile, and bone marrow. By consuming them, whatever life the victim would have had, now belongs to the Raven Mocker.

Eleven-year-old Rutha woke up slowly. She felt Hester, lying next to her squirm and kick in her pre-waking half dream state. However, that was not what woke Rutha. The sound that disturbed her sleep was that of her mother rocking back and forth, back and forth.

The morning sun did not last long as the sky became overcast and dismal as rain threatened. The day reflected Terresse's mood. The horrible nightmare of the Cherokee 'Raven Mocker' left her mind muddled.

What did the nightmare signify? What message did it bring? Was it a warning? Who would even know what the dream meant? Larkin is so far away. Is he in danger? Is the Raven Mocker an omen of Larkin's death?

In some Indian legends, Terresse remembered, a raven is responsible for the origin of humankind and is a guardian spirit. If that was so perhaps, is there one Raven out there to counter the evil Kalann Ahyeliski?

Oh, I wish Mama and Daddy were here. (Jacob and Jane Hammontree, and her brother, Robert with his wife and children left Tennessee for the greener pasture of Missouri before the war).

Larkin brought her to this log cabin as a young bride. They were content with their life and five children. Then, Larkin felt he had to join with his brothers and cousins to defend their way of life.

Tennessee was torn apart as one neighbor favored the Confederates and another the Yankees.

What was this war was about?" Terresse wondered. "Why were the men so anxious to join in the fighting? Even boys seventeen and younger had the fever to fight and volunteered to be soldiers, even drummers, and musicians."

"Yes sir," Granny Raper said on one of her visits. "We'ns is proud to be Tennessean's. Why, we are the state that bred the likes of Andy Jackson, Thomas Merdy, and Davy Crockett. The boys, all of them, Marcus, John, Merdy, Larkin, and James, ain't no different from them, no different at all. They were proud to join in the fight against them Damn Yankees."

"Remember how Larkin and the boys roared with laughter when they recalled Davy's story. They remembered it like it happened yesterday," Granny continued though Terresse was not listening. "Davy became so disgusted with his constituents after losing his seat in Congress that he told them he was going to Texas and declared that the voters of Tennessee could go to hell."

Granny Rutha Hicks Raper often told that the Raper's, Hicks, Hammontree's, and Crockett had often married into each other family.

Terresse's tortured mind whirled in a morass of pain, and a thousand misgivings tore at her heart as Larkin's mother reminisced. She could not bring herself to tell Granny Raper of the Raven Mocker. She doubted the old woman could understand the terror she felt.

"Did you hear the news?" Mrs. Foster, a neighbor, inquired. "General Lee is headed up to Maryland and Pennsylvania. Lee will surely whip them Yankee's up there." Terresse later learned that in early July Lee lost the battle at Gettysburg.

"How could it possibly happen?" Terresse's friend Elizabeth cried. "The whole neighborhood is in shock. Our army lost Vicksburg. I cannot believe the devastating defeat we suffered at Chattanooga. It is another crushing blow."

The long agonizing days and nightmare-plagued nights dragged on

Oh, my love, where are you? Do you have enough food or a warm coat? Are you well or sick?

Oh, the waiting and not knowing, I hate it.

"Conceal some food," Terresse was warned, "against possible seizure and confiscation." Thank god, she had listened to the warning. She and the children butchered a hog, salted it down, and buried the carcass in a barrel. They also stored root vegetables in a pit.

Half dozen battles and hundreds of skirmishes raged on in Tennessee. Terresse barred her door at night and cautioned the children to stay close to home during the day. Cutthroats killed the neighbors down the road. Marauding armies, guerrillas, deserters prowled the countryside. The neighbors whispered that a man had guided bushwhackers, young boys between 14 and 18, to his neighbors' corncribs and beehives. The good men of the town found the traitor, immersed him in honey and hung him from an Oak tree. Terresse's heart ached when Larkin, his brothers, and cousins rode off to fight in the war. Even boys seventeen and younger volunteered to be soldiers even drummers and musicians.

Larkin was a Private with the 39th Tennessee Mounted Infantry Company K while Mexican troops were besieging the Alamo. Davy Crockett, a son of Tennessee, was among the 187 killed at the Alamo. Meanwhile, General Grant held Vicksburg under siege for weeks. Then, on April 17, 1863, Larkin died in the mud and rain of a Mississippi battlefield. Like many of the fallen men, Larkin's body lies in a grave far from his home and loved ones.

> The Southern Soldier Boy
> "A grave in the wood with the grass o'ergrown,
> A grave in the heart of his mother,
> His clay in the one, lifeless, and lone.
> But, his memory lives in the other."

Terresse plaited her hair in one long braid, wound it and pinned it to the back of her neck as usual without looking into the mirror that hung on the wall. She knew that if she looked at her reflection, she would see a woman almost unrecognizable with eyes faded and tragic. She was no longer a vibrant young woman. However, only twenty-seven years old she felt weighed down and old.

"Stop it!" Terresse threw the hairbrush across the room. "Stop feeling sorry for yourself." Playing with her rag doll, Miss Polly Hester jumped and whimpered at the sound of her mother's harsh voice.

"I am sorry. I did not mean to frighten you, baby." She bent down picking the baby up kissing and hugging her tightly, "I am not upset with you little one."

If my Mama were here, Terresse thought, she would scold me. Often, she would tell me to pull myself up by my bootstraps, to get on with my life. Mama would tell me that there are other women worse off than I am. Get on with living, daughter, just plain everyday living.

"You know now what none but widows know," Granny Raper told Terresse. "No one can explain to you these feelings unless they have gone through the ordeal themselves." Yes, Granny knew, a widow since 1815, her husband William had served in the War of 1812. "It is comfortless," Granny, continued shaking her head knowingly. "Yes, it is hard, your widow's life in this torn land, no money, and the care of your five youngens."

"Mama!" eight-year-old Marcus shouted as he came running to the house. "There are some strangers down the road a piece. Don't know if'n they are Yankees or not."

"Rutha, turn the chickens out," Terresse turning to her oldest daughter, "take Hester with you and hide. Marcus, take the boys, the cow, and the mules far out into the woods."

A group of thin, ragged men was pulling up the few vegetables in the garden. Terrified Terresse stood in the doorway. The men crossed the open space and came toward the house.

"Misses," said one of the men who seemed to be the leader. "We haven't eaten for days. Would you have something to spare?"

"I have some rusks." Terresse knew better than to refuse the men. "I will fetch them for you." The children had looked forward to the sweet bread that she had baked that morning. Sweetened with molasses the light, soft textured rusks were a rare treat.

"Thank you kindly, Mam," said the man as she handed him the sack.

"Looky here! Look what we found," someone shouted. Two men were coming out of the woods with a rope around the cow's neck while four chickens hung from their belts.

"That's enough," shouted the first man then turned toward Terresse, "My apologies, Misses."

Thank God, Terresse breathed a sigh of relief after the men walked away down the road.

Marcus found Job and Sally, the two old mules, and led them back to the house. Rutha brought Hester to the house then penned the few chickens that she could find.

War finally ended April 9, 1865, when Lee had surrendered at Appomattox Court House in Virginia. It had been two years, almost to the day, that Larkin had died in the battle of Vicksburg.

"Someday, we will go west," Larkin had once promised her. "We will claim new land, a fertile land, a place where our children can grow tall, strong, and proud."

Now our future is uncertain, Terresse sat down in her rocking chair. We are sure to lose the land we worked so hard on, and the pitiful few possessions we have.

Is it a ridiculous thing to think? Am I losing my mind when I think of picking up and leaving our home? Will we be going toward something or running away?

"Yes," she whispered, "I want to run away from the ghosts, away from the Raven Mocker. I also want to find a better life for the children. It is time. I will close the book on grief and sorrow. It is time to pack away the bitter memories and all the other claptrap."

Will the Raven Mocker leave me alone? Night after night, the nightmare had haunted her.

She walked to the dresser and was still for a few moments as she looked into the dreaded mirror. She felt strength returning to her body. She could feel it in her bones.

"Yes!" She nodded at the apparition reflected there. Now she saw her old image with a glint of determination in her eyes. "I will make Larkin's dream come true."

Hester Louise holding Miss Polly looked curiously at her mother.

"Hester Louise," she picked the baby up twirling around, "How would you like to go west?" The baby giggled gleefully and clapped her hands. She liked this happy mother. "Yes, Hester we will go west to Missouri."

Terresse gathered her children around the table and told them of their father's dream of going west. She was surprised that they so readily accepted the idea of moving. Only Rutha remained silent.

"It will be a real adventure," Marcus exclaimed and let out an Indian war whoop. James and Jacob chimed in with their war whoops.

Terresse sat down that night and wrote to her brother. Dear Robert, the children and I are moving to Missouri. We will leave the first of next month. Please tell Mama and Daddy I love them with affection your sister.

Receiving Robert's answer the family made ready to leave this war-torn, God-forsaken land. The children helped her pull the old battered trunk away from the corner and dusted it off.

"Only the bare necessities," Teressee said while sitting at the table, with the children around her. "I want each of you to think what you want to take on the journey." They were deciding what they should take and what would be packed in the trunk.

"Well, Job and Sally ain't young anymore," Marcus, uttered.

"Job and Sally are not...," corrected Rutha.

"Anyway, they can't pull a heavy load. Ten-year-old Marcus bristled, "I reckon all I need is my gun." Marcus had become an excellent shot. He had learned hunting was a necessity not a sport. With a sharp eye, he often supplied the cooking pot with a squirrel or a rabbit.

"And I have this," Jacob was not to be outdone by his older brother, displayed his slingshot, "so I don't need anything either."

Hester looked up at her mother with a quivering lip, "Miss Polly?"

"Yes, darling, Miss Polly is a part of this family, and we could not possibly think of leaving her behind."

Rutha remained quiet deep in thought.

The family climbed the rugged terrain of the Cumberland Plateau. Job and Sally strained as they pulled the little wagon as it creaked and jarred across the roads deteriorated from the heavy traffic of the armies and animals during the war.

"Mama, what are those?" James asked. Railroad tracks, like so many broken ribs, stood silent monuments to the fallen men both North and

South. There were rails twisted around poles or trees to render them useless.

West, West! They traveled, day by day, following the former 'Trail of Tears' that the Cherokees had traveled almost thirty years before. In 1836, President Andrew Jackson ignored the Supreme Court and ordered the army to remove Indians from their homeland. The army forcibly removed Cherokee, Chickasaw, Choctaws, Creeks, and Seminole and marched them to the 'Indian Territory' set aside in Oklahoma and Kansas. A quarter of the 16,000, Cherokees died during this ordeal.

As the sun edged over a ridge Terresse woke stiff and sore from sleeping on the hard ground. A little shiver ran through her body. She had that dream again. However, this time the Raven Mocker did not devour Larkin's heart. She steeled herself against the tremendous black heartache that threatened to engulf her. Drawing courage into her bones as a thirsty man drinks a cup of cold water she straightened to her full height to face another day.

At daybreak, the boys had made a quick breakfast by thrusting salt pork strips through with a stick, holding it over flames to cook. The meat wrapped in cold biscuits was ready to eat.

Walking beside Job, as usual, a haze of dust hung over the road. Terresse's clothes were permeated with the red powder, enough to sting. The journey had been wearing on all of them especially old Job and Sally. Due to the drought, the stream they were following had been reduced to a trickle. The boys no longer found fish in it.

"Oh Mama," fourteen old Rutha exclaimed a few weeks later. "It is beautiful. I wish we could stay here for a few days. It was a pleasant, shady groove with a flowing stream. I

"Well, we might stay over for just one day." Terresse sympathized with her daughter, and today, even she felt no urge to hurry on. "Yes, I think it might be a good thing. The mules need rest and good grass. We can get some washing done too and you," looking pointedly at the boys, "could use a bath."

"A bath," moaned the boys. Bathing was a luxury on this trip

"I have to admit I truly miss my rocking chair," pressing her hand on her aching back as she stood up when she finished the washing.

The boys dumped armloads of firewood near the campfire. Marcus drove "Y" segments of two large tree branches into the ground, forks up, and laid a pole across them.

"Fire's ready," Marcus called. Terresse was proud that her sons had become resourceful hunting small game. They were adept at building a campfire. They learned to put a few sticks of dry wood into the wagon for the next campsite.

Rutha put a lump of dough into the Dutch oven, covered it with hot coals, and swung it from the pole over the fire to bake.

This is certainly different cooking over an open campfire, Terresse thought. At the fireplace hearth at home I could swing the kettle back and forth on the hook to regulate the cooking temperature.

"Well," Marcus commented dryly, as the children readied for their baths, "they say a little dirt is good for growing children."

"At this rate you will become a giant," Rutha quipped. At this, the children laughed aloud for the first time in many days.

"Tears from laughing so hard have washed my eyes out so I can see," Ruth said.

That night they all slept soundly, and the Raven Mocker did not visit Terresse ever again.

"The weather seems to have changed. It is a little cooler now." Terresse noted the next day as readied to start on their journey.

Terresse smiled as she watched her sons. James is trying so hard, hands in his pockets was stretching to match barefoot step by barefoot step with his brothers as they walked ahead of the wagon.

The children have grown and have uttered little compliant. It seems as though they are the adults and are protecting me. Even old Job feels the raising spirits of the children. He has a spring in his step.

Four-year-old Hester, holding a worn Miss Polly in her left arm and a much-used right thumb in her mouth, had snuggled down into the quilts in the wagon for a nap.

My poor baby, Terresse thought, she has learned that her Mama does not have time to pamper her. I must soon mend Miss Polly before she falls apart.

"Mama, tell me again what Uncle Robert wrote in his letter," Marcus requested that night. Although, he had assumed the role of 'man-of-the-family', occasionally reverted to an inquiring boy. "You know the part about how Missouri got its name." Marcus wanted to be like his Uncle Mark Raper and go to Texas someday. Uncle Mark was one of the TEXAS INDIAN FIGHTERS in that far away land that had claimed Davy Crockett.

One time Uncle Mark wrote, Captain Hays is very particular as to the kind of men he enlisted, and that is one reason why he has the best set of Indian fighters, taken as a whole, which Texas ever produced. A man has to have courage, good character, be a good rider, a good shot, and have a horse worth $100. In my company, which is the first company, are Wallace, Woolford, Joe Tivey, Kit Ackland, Jim Galbreth, Tom Buchanan, Coho Jones, Peter Poe, Mike Chevalier, and Ad Gillespie."

"Well, son," Terresse said, "Robert said that the name was---."

"Uncle Robert said that it was an Al---, Al---," stammered Jacob trying to get a grip on the big word.

"Algonquin," corrected Rutha, ever the schoolteacher to her siblings. "Uncle Robert said that Missouri is a name for the Algonquin Indians that lived near the mouth of the river."

"Are there still wild Indians there?" James asked. James remembered the tales told in the family about Granny Raper's experience, how the frenzied Indians scalped and killed, in the early days when the family settled in North Carolina and Tennessee. "Will they scalp us?"

"Of course not," Marcus answered patting his trusty rifle. "I will protect you anyhow. I bet Uncle Robert must have wiped them Indians out by now."

"Mama, will it be like—like home?" The thought had worried Rutha often. However, she had not asked her mother before.

Terresse saw the worried look on her daughters face. Rutha's bonnet had slid back onto her neck. Terresse had often cautioned her daughter. However, it usually up around her neck with her curls springing from her braids.

"Oh Rutha, I am sure it will be better. Remember that Robert wrote that his children go to school. I am sure that you will have a chance to go to school."

"School, who needs school," Marcus muttered. Jacob and James heartily agreed.

One morning they heard Marcus shouting, "Mama!" He was jumping up and down pointing to the west.

"Mama, is that the Mississippi?" Terrasse's hands calloused, but still beautiful, a Queen's hand, shaded her eyes, as she took in the awe-inspiring panorama of the mighty Mississippi River. She choked back tears. "Yes son that is the Mississippi and on the other side is Missouri."

Robert had promised that he would be at Cape Girardeau to meet them on the first of the month. He would escort them the rest of the way to his home near Springfield.

Terresse discovered that the State of Missouri required her to take a test oath to bar Confederate sympathizers from holding public office, voting, teaching, practicing law and preaching.

"We will take the oath," Terresses' father told her, "But as for myself I will take that oath only from the teeth out."

Terresse patted her hair and straightened her bonnet and hesitantly entered the Court House. After inquiring where she should go, she waited in front of a man sitting behind a desk. He looked self-important, rather pleased with himself. The man was short and stocky, well, not stocky but downright fat. His face was red, and he had bristling red hair, what there was of it.

After a seemly unnecessary long wait, the man stood up, strutted, as he walked to face Terresse. His clothes were a significant check pattern. "Raise your right hand and repeat after me: *I do solemnly swear, that I am well acquainted with the terms of the third section of the second Article of the Constitution of the State of Missouri ---*"

Would God punish her for lying?

"Speak up woman; I can't hear you." The fat man chided Terresse. His breath revolted her. She straightened and looked down on the man's bald head and continued to speak.

"*---adopted in the year eighteen hundred and sixty-five and have carefully considered the same, that I have never, directly or indirectly, done any of the acts in said section specified, that I have always been truly and loyally on the side of the United States against all enemies thereof, foreign and domestic, that I will bear true faith and allegiance to the United States and will support the Constitution and law thereof, as the supreme law of the land, foreign and* *domestic, that I will bear true faith and allegiance to the United States and will support the Constitution and laws **thereof**, as the supreme law of the land,"*

The man droned on while Terresse repeated the oath.

"any law and ordinance of any State to the contrary notwithstanding; that I will to the best of ability, protect and defend the Union of the United States, and not allow the same to be broken up and dissolved, or the Government thereof to be destroyed or overthrown, under any circumstances, if in my power to prevent it; that I will support the Constitution of the State of Missouri; and that I make this oath without any mental reservation or evasion, and hold it to be binding on me." (13), (14), (15)

The smell of the man's foul breath and the taste of the oath in her mouth gagged her.

She left the loathsome man and exited the courthouse. She climbed into the wagon eager to get away from the town. She whipped up Job and Sally to a fast trot. The breeze from the fast pace of her horse calmed her, she started humming and then sang

> *"The homespun dress is plain I know, my hats, palmetto too;*
> *But then it shows what Southern girls from Southern rights will do.*
> *We send the bravest of our land to battle with the foe,*
> *And we will lend a helping hand, we love the South, you know."*
> *Hurrah! Hurrah!*
> *For the sunny South, so dear;*
> *Three cheers for the homespun dress*
> *The Southern ladies wear!*

The people in this story are my real ancestors. Terresse and Larkin are my great-grandparents. How Terresse made the trip from Tennessee to Missouri, I do not know. I let my imagination soar at that point.

Terresse never married again. *Terresse Ellen Hammontree Raper*
7 Nov 1826 - 22 Sep 1896
Buried: Slagle Cemetery, Polk County, Missouri

Kalanu Ahkyeliski, (cah-lah-noo awk-yee-lee-ss-kee) Raven Mocker
Tennessee is a name that comes from the word TANASI of the

Cherokee language. It also is a name of an Indian village on the Little Terresse River.

Total deaths exceeded 600,000 and the dead and wounded combined totaled about 1.1 million. There were more Americans killed in the Civil war than in all other American wars combined from the colonial period through the later phase of the Vietnam War (1950-1975). (12)

Jacob Asbury Hammontree
A great-great grandfather.
Pvt. 1 Reg't (Wear's) East Tenn Vols War of 1812
Born: 3 April 1790 in Lincoln, North Carolina
Died: 21 July 1865
Burial: Slagle Cemetery, Polk County, Missouri U.S.A

Terresse's father, Jacob Asbury Hammontree was born in 1790 in Lincoln County, North Carolina the child of William Hammontree and Pats Hawkins. He had two sons and seven daughters with his wife Jane between 1816 and 1833. Jacob, age 22, served in the military during the War of 1812. That war claimed the lives of 15,000 soldiers.

Apparently, Jacob was living in Missouri, around the time when pro-slavery and anti-slavery forces clashed along the Kansas-Missouri border. Jacob's father, William, passed away about 1815, at the age of 65 and his mother, Patsy, also passed about 1815.

5

JACOB ASBURY RAPER/RAPIER
A GRANDFATHER

Jacob born on June 22, 1855, in Monroe County, Tennessee was a son of Larkin Webb and Tennessee (Hammontree) Raper.

After fourteen years of marriage, Jacob was devastated when Delilah passed away on June 19, 1887. Jacob buried his beloved wife near Fairlane, Ottawa, Oklahoma. About this time familylore is that one of the women in the family thought that RAPER was not refined enough, so the family name became RAPIER. However, the name, in England, was spelled as Raper, Rapier, Roper, and Rooper. The word Raper meant rope maker. Many were involved with ships and shipping of goods and slaves.

The Civil war or the War of Rebellion, depending on your perspective, still stirred strong feelings and constant reminders of the bitter, long-lasting resentments that kept many old wounds festering. These were the turbulent years of the James' and Younger' gangs, when the Miller and Ford brothers and Quantrill rode throughout the countryside raising hell were still fresh in the minds of the people.

Jacob was thirty-five when he married his second wife, Josephine Virginia Hall, my grandmother, January 30, 1890, in Springfield, Greene, Missouri. Josie was born to Thomas and Margaret Hall March 17, 1860, in Carroll County, Arkansas.

Turmoil must have crept into the heart of Josephine's father, Thomas Greene Hall when his daughter married into a Confederate family. Thomas had served in the Union Army as a private with Company B, 24th Missouri

Infantry for three years. Perhaps the men who shared the shared legacy of the war may have healed their psychological scars.

Thomas was born on January 16, 1833, in Calloway County, Kentucky to Richard and Nancy Hall. When he was 20, he married Margaret Catherine Atkinson on December 25, 1853.

MARGARET & THOMAS HALL
Battle of Pea Ridge,
He told of one in-

Thomas Hall was in the Battle of Pea Ridge near Elkhorn Tavern, Benton County, Arkansas. The battle was described by one Union Officer this way:

Great God what a scene is presented. The mangled trunks of men are thickly scattered around. From each tree or sheltering rock, the groans of the wounded arise. Muskets, saddles, horses, blankets, hats, and clothes hang on every bush, or in gory manner stew on the ground. And now in the valley to the right ten thousand cheers proclaim victory ours. Dead horses, dead men, and dismounted guns are strewed over the blood-drenched field, and as some gun is taken or trophy secured, renewed cheering and shouts of gladness ring out upon the air.

Lyman Bennett—March 8, 1962

The Battle of Pea Ridge lasted from March 6 through 8, 1862. The Union commander was Samuel R. Curtis, and the Confederate Commander was Earl Van Dorn. There were 10,500 Union troops and 16,000 Confederate troops. Estimated casualties were 1,349 Union men and 4,600 Confederate men.

It is likely that Thomas received medical care. Jessie Mae, a bouncing baby girl, Jacob's third daughter, was born to this union June 5, 1896. Jacob's mother, Terresse Ellen, passed away that same year, at sixty-nine, on September 22, 1896, in Polk County, Missouri. It was an exciting period in history as in 1898, the Holland, the first practical submarine, was launched. Hawaii was annexed to the United States. Also, the Supreme Court permitted the existence of separate educational facilities for black and white students. My father, Clarence Thomas, Jacob's fifth son, the first by Josie, was born May 13, 1899, in Springfield, Greene, Missouri. Jacob was 43 and Josephine was 39. Thomas had softened somewhat toward his son-in-law when this second grandchild was born.

In 1900 the family lived in Springfield, Ward 5, Greene, Missouri.

Daddy was never sure what year he was born. The year 1896 was on many of his legal papers including his World War I military records. His discharge, May 25, 1918, states that he was 24 years old when he was actually 19. A few years later while researching the family, I found the 1900 U. S. Census, which lists Dad as an infant. Also, my mother and I were on a visit to Missouri in 1957 when we discovered more evidence in an old family bible owned by Mr. John Phillips. In that Bible, the year of my father's birth was May 13, 1899

The Phillips family married into the Hall family decades earlier. Mr. Phillips and his son, also named John, were two gracious old men who lived together. They graciously welcomed us into their home. The only indoor plumbing they had was a water pump in the kitchen.

Dad's birth was recorded in their Bible as May 12, 1899. Six days after Daddy's third birthday, May 19, 1902, mother, Josephine Virginia, died.

"The only memory I have of my mother," my father told me, "Mama had wrapped me in a brightly colored quilt and rocked me. I remember the clean scent of soap in her raven hair that hung long, thick, and wavy about her shoulders."

"Josephine's grandson Leonard, Jessie's' oldest boy, wrote to me years later that his mother, Jessie Mae, told him that her mother had fallen down a flight of stairs, which was fatal to both her and her unborn child." Jessie would have been about five and one-half years old at the time of her mother's death and may have witnessed the tragedy.

(The Springfield Republican newspaper Obit notice, May 22, 1902 page 5. Mrs. Josie V. Raper, who died on May 19 at 219 East Division street Springfield, MO, will be interred in the Brighton cemetery today, the 21st.

Jacob about the time he married Delilah.

Jacob's oldest son, George Rapier

Jacob's son, Floyd Rapier

Floyd Rapier wearing his Derby hat

I do not have a photo of Jacob's first wife, Delilah Gorman Long.

Jacob's wife #2 Josephine Virginia Hall. My Grandmother.

Jacob, Josephine and daughter Jessie.

∽ 6 ∾

CLARENCE THOMAS, TOMMY. RAPIER
MY FATHER

ote: During his childhood, my father, Clarence Thomas Rapier's was called Tommy.

A gathering of churchwomen came to the Hall home to wash and dress Josie for burial.

"Don't stir yourself," the woman was peering through thick lenses of her spectacles at Margaret Hall. Tommy, hiding behind his Grandmother's chair, was transfixed. The fat woman's glasses had a magnifying effect on her eyes, which reminded him of a huge bug.

"We will take care of everything that needs doing," twittering like a bird; a tiny woman patted Margaret's arm. As the long hot afternoon wore on many of the women had gone home. But the fat woman lingered.

The fat woman had lingered behind with a sly smile she said, "Margaret, I would be pleased to have Josie's ring as a memento,"

Jacob enters the room just then and overheard the woman's remark. He flared up at the woman's audacity.

"NO! That ring stays on Josie's finger where it belongs."

Jacob hustled the woman to the door.

"Well," she indignantly muttered under breath, "after all I have done for that family."

That evening only one lamp burned in the far corner of the parlor.

Tommy and Jessie

Tommy climbed up on a chair, his eyes round with wonder as he stared at his Mama's face. His Mama had delicate, beautiful high cheekbones, but why were they so white. The scent of lavender soap still clung to her hair. Their special quilt lay across his Mama's feet. Why was his Mama lying in that funny bed that was on the dining room chairs?

"Mama, wake up," Tommy pleaded. "Mama, please wake up."

"Brothers and Sisters fall to your knees," the preacher instructed the next day, "while I petition the Lord upon his children's behalf."

As the Preacher droned on Jessie developed an intense dislike for the man.

He talks as if Mama is a sinner, Jessie thought, *I know Mama is not a sinner. Daddy told me Mama is in Heaven with the baby.*

The preacher prayed a long, long time. Tommy was tired and his knees hurt from kneeling so long he shifted his weight from one knee to the other.

"Tommy, stop that wiggling," Grandmother scolded.

"Good afternoon," Tipping his hat as Jacob greeted a man and his wife on the street. Tommy holding his father's hand saw that the woman was the same one with the bug eyes. Jacob exchanged a few tidbits of news with the husband when the woman's nervous hands drew his attention. She was twisting a ring round and round her finger. The ring looked familiar. Astonishment swept over Jacob when he realized the truth.

"That's Josie's ring!" shouted Jacob as he lunged toward the woman grabbing her hand trying to remove the ring from her finger.

"E-e-eh-," the woman shrieked and fainted in her husband's arms. They both ended on the ground, she pinning her Lilliputian husband beneath her.

"If you don't give me that ring I will tear your finger off," Jacob threatened as he loomed over them. The woman squeaked like a frightened rabbit.

"Someone, go get the police," the words escaped with a spray of salvia from the husband's mouth. A crowd was gathering, and soon a police officer arrived.

"Calm down Jacob," the police officer who had responded to the uproar was a friend of Jacob's; however, he had no choice but to take them to the jailhouse.

"The only way to settle this matter," the Judge pronounced, "since each person claims the ring, is to exhume Mrs. Raper, to prove or disprove the claims."

Men shoveled the dirt from Josie's grave then brushed off the last layer from the top of the casket. The assemblage held their breath and leaned close.

"OH. MY. GOD!" Horrified at what met his eyes Jacob's knees buckled. Women screamed. The fat woman fainted. No one tried to catch her as she fell to the ground. Josie in her coffin had strands of long, dark hair were in her fists. Her fingernails were broken and bloodied from scraping on her coffin. The ring was missing from her finger.

⌒ A MEMOIR OF THE RAPIER'S ⌒

The doctor pronounced, "Josephine must have been in a deep coma, and we were not aware of it."

Jacob collapsed at the gravesite.

A few weeks later Jacob was released from the hospital. The first thing he did was to gather Jessie and Tommy to him hugging them tightly.

"Your Mama is gone and ---." Jacob could not continue.

Why are there tears in his Papa's eyes? Tommy had never seen his Papa cry. Snuggling closer to his Papa, the familiar scent of tobacco soothed him.

"Where did Mama go?" Tommy puzzled. Mama never left him before.

"Oh, Tommy your Mama---," Jacob could not get the rest of the words out. First Delilah, now Josie.

"Will Mama be back tomorrow?"

"No Tommy," six-year-old Jessie answered her brother, "God took her to Heaven."

Tommy had never seen anything that had died before except a baby bird that had fallen out of the nest. He did not think that the bird had gone to heaven because it had lain under the tree for a long time until Jessie buried it. "Mama," he started to cry, "Mama."

Jacob battled his short-term memory loss from the shock of seeing his wife's body. He could not remember the dates of his children's birth.

"Jacob, Jessie, and Tommy will be better off staying with a relative for the time being," the doctor advised, "at least, until you are capable of caring for your children."

Tommy and Jessie stayed with various relatives for a time, usually with Uncle Larkin (James) or Aunt Rutha Jane Crockett.

Grandmother Hall sat in her rocking chair while the children kneeled on the floor near her.

"Tell us a story," the children begged. Their little grandmother was an excellent storyteller.

"What story shall I tell you?" Margaret placed her finger to her forehead, "I know, I will tell you the story in the Cherokee lore about Brave Eagle."

(Brave Eagle and Little Fawn: - from War Eagle – Cherokee Myths and Legions.)

"Once upon a time," Margaret smiled and started. *"There was a mighty*

warrior whose name was Brave Eagle. Brave Eagle ventured far from home on a vision quest. One morning he woke up to hauntingly beautiful singing. He followed the music to a grassy glen. There he saw a young Indian maiden dancing and singing by a bubbling brook. As he watched the girl dance and sing, he fell in love with her."

"Brave Eagle captured the maiden and took her home with him. Giant Dew Eagle, the bringer of rain, could not find his daughter Little Fawn. Giant Dew Eagle became so sad that he caused a great drought to come upon the earth. From that time Little Fawn sang only sad songs and would not dance."

"Little Fawn cried every day as if her heart would break. In sympathy with Little Fawn, West Wind roared so loudly that Sun turned away and Sky hid its face in the clouds and wept." Tommy put his hands over his face and crept closer to Jessie.

"Brave Eagle's heart was touched by Little Fawn's sorrow. He asked Little Fawn what he could do to make her sing with happiness again. Little Fawn cried that she missed her home. Brave Eagle vowed on his honor that he would take Little Fawn back to her home if he only knew the way."

"Hooray," shouted Jessie.

"Hearing Brave Eagle's vow the God of Thunder opened the sky, and Wind Lord blew Brave Eagle and Little Fawn to Little Fawn's home in the sky where her father, Giant Dew Eagle greeted his daughter, but he threatened to kill Brave Eagle for taking his daughter."

"Oh no," groaned the children.

"Little Fawn stopped her father and told him that she had come to love Brave Eagle for he had shown her gentleness and kindness but that she knew she could not marry him without permission from Kitshi Manito's permission for their marriage."

"Kitshi Manito?" Jessie frowned at the name.

"Kitshi Manito said that Brave Eagle might become a member of Little Fawn's Cherokee family, but first he would set Brave Eagle a task."

"Brave Eagle," said Kitshi Manito, "you shall bring back tokens from all the animals of the forest, or you shall not marry Little Fawn. If you accomplish this feat, I will know that the animals of the forest agree that you, Brave Eagle, are a brave and worthy warrior."

"Wind Lord carried Brave Eagle back to earth. Brave Eagle sought out all the animals n the forest. Bear for his strength, Panther for his stealth, Fox for his cunning, Deer for his timidity, Trout for his grace and beauty. Then Brave Eagle looked to the sky and begged Eagle, his totem, for his token."

"Brave Eagle returned to Kitshi Manito and laid the tokens from all the animals before the master of the earth. Kitshi Manito found that Brave Eagle had the approval of all the animals in the forest. Kitshi Manito married Brave Eagle and Little Fawn."

"The Spirit of Summer blessed the young warrior and his wife with fertility, and Giant Dew Eagle caused the rain to return to the earth. Brave Eagle and Little Fawn had a baby boy. From that day Little Fawn taught all of her children to dance and sing with happiness."

Jessie and Tommy clapped their hands for the happy conclusion of Brave Eagle and Little Fawn. "Now it is time for bed." The children were not sleepy but obeyed their Grandmother.

Entering now was Miss Ann Beal who applied for the job of caring for Tommy and Jessie.

"This woman is not what I had in mind." Jacob thought as he looked at the young woman. *"I want a more grandmotherly type. However,* Miss Beal appears to be capable, and she lived nearby within walking distance. Jacob was in desperate straits, so he hired the young woman.

Jacob was once again a widower with young children, who needed attention and motherly care. The solution was to marry again. Such marriages were for practical purposes. Seven months after Josie's death, Jacob and Maud were married on December 21, 1902.

Twenty-three-year-old Maud Ann Beal became forty-seven-year-old Jacob Rapier's third wife. They eventually had four children: Ruby Lane, Lulu Marjorie (Sis), Paul Jacob, and Marshall Clair.

Of Tommy's older brothers, George, Floyd, Willie and Elmer, I believe from the stories Daddy told me Floyd must have been his favorite. *Daddy told us a story, whether a tall-tale or not, this is what he said.* "Floyd was quite a character. Two women on a train entered into a conversation, as their husbands both worked for the railroad. They apparently had much in common, although they lived at the opposite ends of the track. They bragged about their families showing photographs. They were startled to discover they were married to the same man. Floyd!" "Please tell us a story," Tommy begged when Floyd came to visit

Well," drawled Floyd ever the kidder and full of fun, *"there was once a turtle who could whistle. He could whistle better than anyone. All the animals in the forest were amazed at the beautiful songs he whistled."* Floyd puckered up and whistled 'Johnny Came Marching Home.' Tommy tried to imitate his brother. However, he could not whistle.

Note: Daddy never did learn to whistle except what in later years I called it Dad's whisper-whistle.

"Quit being a pest and let Floyd tell the story," demanded Jessie

"Well one day, Quail asked to see Turtle's whistle. The turtle was so kindhearted that he agreed. Quail flew to the top of a dogwood tree where he taunted Turtle and laugh at him."

"That was no nice," Jessie huffed.

"Well now, Turtle realized that he would never get his whistle back."

"I bet I could get the whistle back for Turtle," Tommy bragged.

"Hush," Jessie was getting upset at Tommy's interruptions.

"Quail had outfoxed little-kindhearted Turtle and Turtle was afraid that his friends would laugh at him too. From that day, Turtle lost his confidence. That is why Turtle hides in his house that he carries on his back." "I was about three or four," Daddy vividly recalled, "when my brother, Floyd took me to town. We saw a crowd gathering in the square." The atmosphere that the young boy saw before him was almost carnival-like. "Floyd swung me up onto his shoulders and put his derby hat on my head."

"I heard men laughing and shouting. They were pushing and shoving a Negro with a rope around his neck. They hung that fellow. The body looked so little swinging back and forth from that cottonwood tree." Floyd quick as possible hustled me away from the scene. From then on; every time I passed that tree, I could feel cold shivers running up and down my back."

"Daddy was devastated when he received word that Floyd had died while working on the railroad May 15, 1912."

Years later, my oldest sister Josephine, who lived in Elkland, Missouri, wrote to me, 'Springfield will still have something in the paper each year about the incident.'

At one time, upon entering Greene County, Missouri, a sign warned black people: **"Nigger! Don't let the sun set on you in this county."**

This was not the only place that sported a sign of like manner. Posted in Dalhart, Texas a sign read, **"Black Man! Don't Let the Sun Go Down On You Here."**

The withdrawal of federal troops from the South in 1877 effectively ended Reconstruction and protection for African Americans. New laws and penal systems enforced many restrictions, and vigilantes often took the law into their hands.

Between 1882 and 1900 there were at least 100 blacks lynched a year. The record year was 1892. Lynched were one hundred and sixty-one African Americans.

In the 1890's African American journalist, Ida Wells Barnett initiated a campaign to make people aware of the lynching and prevent it. Ms. Barnett headed the Anti-lynching Bureau of the National Afro-American Council. This council proved that most of the lynching was not the outcome of rape or attempted rape. Victims were lynched for outspokenness, and lynching was a device used to frighten and intimidate African Americans both politically and socially.

Jacob eventually owned a ranch in which the house stood in Kansas while the outhouse and corals were across the state line in Oklahoma. Jacob soon acquired a few good horses that he would race."

"Good girl," Jacob said as his hands ran down the withers of his prize filly. "You are a real lady." The tall bay was a beautiful animal. Jacob's older sons, George, Floyd, Willie, and Elmer, got in the habit of feeding the horse, raw eggs, which made her coat gleam.

The boys matched their father in height and strength. Under their tutelage, Tommy became an excellent rider. The boys affectionately called their little brother Tommy and elected him to put the horse through its paces. About this time, the family had stables just a block west of where the Springfield Court House sits today.

ARLENE JANOSKI

Jacob with his sons: Elmer, Clarence, George, Paul and Marshall.

When Dad was riding the racehorses, at that time, was about the same age then as his youngest stepbrother, Marshall, in the photo above.

"We won several races," Daddy recalled and explained the procedure. "I would whisper in the bay's ear and pat her neck to calm her. George stood at the starting point to urge the horse on, and Floyd or one of them was at the finish line to help bring the horse to a halt in case I couldn't stop her." "One day Dad and Maud went to town leaving Jessie and me alone," Daddy chuckled, "Well, I caught a skunk and killed it. I put it in the oven to render out the fat to use for greasing some of the harnesses. When they came home, I was working in the field. That night Daddy commented that was a good rabbit I had in the oven. I never told him what he had eaten."

"I never got along with Maud," Daddy told us. "She would whip me for various reasons. She would sprinkle salt on the bed saying that it would burn and make me stop wetting the bed. She often called me a little nigger, taunting me about my dark hair and skin."

Note: My father always said that his mother had enough Cherokee blood that she was entitled to a 'Head Right.' We children grew up being proud of that heritage. "An uncle claimed it for his children," he said. "They got a college education while Jessie and I got not one dime."

When Tommy was a boy, it was still considered a disgrace to be Indian.

Note: In 2015, I had a DNA test. I was sorely disappointed to find I had no Indian blood at all. I must admit that to this day I have not discovered evidence of any Indian blood. My DNA is 53% European West, 33% Irish, 3% Iberian Peninsula, and 3% other according to Ancestry.com.

One cold winter day the Matthews family was shocked when they discovered ten-year-old Tommy lying on the wooden walkway in front of the general store in Liberal, Kansas. Perhaps this is the first time Tommy had run away from home. Nevertheless, Jacob and Maud had moved once again and for an unknown reason left him behind.

"I had a high fever and delirious. Mrs. Matthews nursed me back to health. They treated me just like a son of their own. I became good friends with her son who was my age."

"Here boys are some new shirts for you," called Mrs. Matthews. She had cut two shirts in half. One was blue the other red, and then she sewed a red half to the blue and a blue half to the red. "Well, I guess I will be able to tell you apart from a distance now." That was funny because he was shorter than I was and blond.

"Well boys, it is time for a haircut," Mrs. Matthews announced. "You boys look like a couple of wild mustangs. I sat still on a stool in the yard and watched the chickens roaming around my feet while Mrs. Matthews cut my hair with a straight razor. I was afraid that she would slip and cut my throat."

When I was thirteen years old Dad asked me if I would cut his hair. He was bald at that time and using his straight razor started on the back. I kept trying to even the hairline on his neck out and was cutting higher and higher. Finally, Dad told me it was good enough and I did a swell job.

"We boys decided to find some wild grapes to eat, but first we weighed ourselves to see if we would gain weight after eating the grapes. However, all we got for our trouble was our faces smeared with grape juice and a tummy ache. We looked like we had Indian Warpaint on."

Bullet wagged his white tail with anticipation waiting while Tommy saddled his horse.

"Come on Bullet," Tommy called. "Get up here." Bullet jumped up behind his boy. Bracing on the saddle Bullet put his paws on his boy's shoulders then licked the boy's ears making him laugh.

"This is how Bertha Kaepernick does it," Tommy shouted at his friend. Bertha was a trick rider at the 101 Ranch. The 101 was a ranch, farm, and headquarters for the cowboys who made up the Oklahoma Show business contingent of the early 1900's. The ranch was located a few miles south of Ponca City, Oklahoma in the north-central part of the state. It went out of business in 1931.

Riding as if he were part of the horse, sticking to it like a tick, Tommy demonstrated. With the reins in his hands, he stood upright on the backs of the horses as they in tandem, galloped around the corral. His left leg braced on the back of one horse, and his right leg is bending with the rhythm and movement of the other horse, Roman-style.

Tommy stayed with the Matthews for a time until his father came to get him.

"I started shaving (with a straight-razor) when I was about twelve-years-old to make himself appear a few years older."

"One day Maud caught me shaving with Daddy's razor. She whipped me with the razor strop until my legs bled. I ran away from home. It was not the first time I ran away. I worked at several ranches in Colorado and Oklahoma."

"I loved my horse. He was well trained and dependable. I rolled my cigarettes and occasionally took a chew from a plug of tobacco, intimidating the other wranglers." Through his teen years, Tommy became a full-fledged, wild and woolly cowboy. He was also a trick rider and bronc buster.

Most of the cowhands had known Tommy since he was knee-high to a Grasshopper and nicknamed him 'Blacky.'

"Well Tommy," the boss chuckled when he noticed the boys nicked up face, "It looks like you have grown up a mite since I last seen you. Reckon I can use a top hand. Anybody that can ride like you and is old enough to shave can work for me."

As a young boy Tommy worked on several ranches in Oklahoma, Kansas, and Colorado.

"Ride 'em, Blacky," the men shouted encouragement. "Ride 'em."

The mustang sunfished, Tommy almost lost his seat.

"Yes sir," spoke up one of the wranglers hanging over the rail to watch the performance, "you can bet that Blacky knows a horse from nose to tail, inside and out, backward and forward. He can break the Broncos the quick way by riding them until they gave out." However, Tommy would break them Indian style, the gentle way.

The Mustang once again turned his belly to the sun.

"Show him who the boss is," the foreman shouted.

"At one ranch we fellows spied the boss's daughter desperately trying to stay in her saddle. We raced after her. I could see her hanging by her belt that was caught on the saddle horn. She was being beaten to death against the fence line. We were to late to save her. We figured that her horse had been startled by a rattlesnake."

"At another ranch, the boss had built a play house for his children on the bank of the Cimarron River. The children took turns pretending to be General Custer, Crazy Horse, or their favorite gunfighters like Doc Holliday and Wyatt Earp. One of the girls would be Belle Starr."

"A summer thunderstorm loomed over the distant mountains. An unexpected torrent of muddy and turbulent water rushed down a canyon and on into the river causing a flash flood, which washed away numerous houses."

"The children were in the playhouse when the flood hit. I helped with the search, but never found the children or the playhouse."

"I started working for the Miller Brothers who owned the 101 Ranch in Oklahoma. There was a captive black bear named Tony at their ranch. I felt sorry for Tony since he was usually secured with a stout chain in front of the ranch house or else he was in an old gorilla cage. Tony dug a cave under the sidewalk where he stays when is either hot or cold.

Note: Tony was given to the Miller's by William "Bill" McFadden after a hunting trip in Mississippi.

That cage sometimes served as a jail for a salty cowboy or two,"

"Tony loved soda pop. He would slurp it right down while holding the bottle in his paws." Tony drinks the pop by the case. People would pay 5 Cents at the Ranch store then give to Tony. They did not realize how they were abusing the poor bear. Tony weighed 800 pounds as an adult. He died in 1931 from a kidney ailment probably caused by the soda pop. (17)

"Say that kid can sure ride." a man in a Derby hat commented. He was watching while the men were encouraging Tommy.

"Let her rip," one cowboy shouted. "Show that bronc who's the boss."

"Like a wild Indian," the foreman answered the man.

Later the man approached Tommy, "Say, young man, what you would say to a job riding and doing your tricks in a circus?"

"I joined the 101's Show and Circus about 1914," Daddy recalled. "I was signed on as a trick rider. While I worked there, I met Tom Mix and Will Rodgers."

"In 1929 and 1930, our family lived in Ponca City, Oklahoma. Daddy took his children to the 101 Ranch where they saw Tony, the bear, as well as Tom Mix, the movie star, who performed at the rodeo on his white horse, also named Tony."

"We saw a Buffalo," Eugene recalled, "who got a leg broke and had to be hauled away on a sled by a team of horses."

Tom Mix was in a series of wild-west shows and featured in many movies with Tony, his wonder horse. Will Rodgers was an American cowboy, comedian, humorist, social commentator, vaudeville performer, and an actor.

Rodgers was born in a prominent Cherokee Nation family in Indian Territory (now part of Oklahoma).

Rodgers once said, "When I die, my epitaph, or whatever you call those signs on gravestones, is going to read: "I looked about every prominent man of my time, but I never met a man I didn't like." I am so proud of that; I can hardly wait to die so it can be carved."

A story that Daddy told his children many times: "Tom Mix, Will Rodgers, my brother Floyd married sisters."

Which of Mix's five wives was one of the sisters? Tom (Thomas Hezekiah) Mix married (1) Mabel Hubbard War, (2) Victoria Ford, (3) Kitty Jewel Perinne, (4) Grace I. Allin, and (5) Olive Stokes.

The men and women of the 101 Ranch and Circus.

"Floyd made two braided, leather, lariats," Daddy told us. The lariat measured sixty feet long and 3/8 of an inch thick. "Floyd gave one of the ropes to Tom Mix and kept the other. Floyd's rope was given to me after he died." A grandson has it now. A granddaughter inherited Daddy's prized saddle, which at one time was worth more than a horse.

William "Will" Penn Adair Rodgers married Betty Blake.

The 101 Circus and Wild West Show played in many small towns between St. Louis, and Bill Pickett was another character that Tommy watched many times, from the top fence rail breaking horses and bulldogging for the show tours in 1912 and 1917. (18)

"Bill Pickett, was a colored fellow," stated Bill King, "who instigated the bulldogging work for the 101."

Note: Bill King was a rancher in Kim, Colorado and rodeo performer in early 1900. 'Kim Yesterday and Today' by Ella Mae Yocam and Edith Anderson was published by the Kim School Community Association

The Miller brothers went on the road with their show; when they were showing in El Paso, they went across to Juarez (Mexico) to see a bullfight. I guess they were doing a little drinking and "hob-nobbing" with the upper-class Mexicans over there who were telling how great their bullfights were."

"We've got a man who can just about kill one of those steers," one of the Miller boys said, "and throw him in the dust. The Mexicans bet $1,000 he couldn't. Well, Pickett did. He went down on him and got that bugger, and twisted him down, and that's where bulldogging started."

"Yes sir, it was quite a sight to see Pickett bulldogging," Daddy told us. "Pickett would grab hold of a horn with one hand, twist an ear with the other, and then he would bite the bull's nose or lip to force the bull down. He would have that steer on the ground before you could blink."

Note: When Daddy told the Pickett story in his later years to the grandchildren, some found it hard to believe but never expressed their opinion aloud. Years later, after Daddy died, a program on PBS television station aired the story of Bill Pickett. So much for the skeptics!

May 1912, the Miller brothers gathered a group to perform in England. The company included Zack Miller, Johnny Baker, Buffalo Bill Cody's 'adopted' son.

Some of the entertainers in the show were a group of Indians, Bill Pickett, Guy Weadick, Florence La Due, Milt Hinkle, George Hooker, Ruth Roach, Mable Clive, Lottie Shaw, Chester Byers, Fred and Ed Burns, Lottie Aldridge, Stack Lee, Jane Fuller, Hank Durnell, Lucille Mann, Alice Lee, Babe Willets, and Dot Vernon.

"The 101 Show arrived in New York," daddy told us, "and while we were boarding the ship that was to take us to England, I saw a big man coming up the gang-plank, his hat with a wide brim, was low on his brow. No one else had a gait like that except my father."

"Come on son it's time to head for home," He told me. I did not put up an argument, although I was disappointed at not making the trip. "The world's Greatest Wild West Show performance was given in front of British nobles and European monarchs such as King George V and Queen Mary; King George's mother Queen Alexander; and her sister the Dowager Empress Marie of Russia. (20)

In 1914, the revolution was raging in Mexico and World War I broke out while the 101 Show and Circus were playing in England. The allies in 1914 were Great Britain, France, and USSR. The enemies were the Axis Powers: Germany, Italy, and Japan.

England impressed the show's animals, vehicles, and wagons into service for which, the Miller brothers received the equivalent of eighty thousand dollars.

Many of the Royalty that had sat together cheering and clapping, and enjoying the World's Greatest Wild West Show became avowed enemies as World War I broke out.

Creditors closed the Wild West Show on September 16, 1931, after the ranch suffered a net loss of the equipment of eighty thousand dollars. A grand era was lost forever when the 101 Ranch passed from the Miller's hands. (20)

The Strawberry Roan *(21)* Note: A roan is a reddish horse with white or gray hairs.

> *Well, it's oh that strawberry roan, Oh, that strawberry roan!*
> *I'll bet all my money the man ain't alive*
> *That can stay with old strawberry when he*
> *makes his high dive. Oh, that strawberry roan!*

The J.J. Cattle Company, a power in the country, ran from Higbe, south of La Junta, Colorado to twenty-five miles southeast of Kim in the McArthur Community. It had approximately 15,000 cattle grazing in an area fifty miles long and at least thirty miles wide south of the Arkansas River in Las Animas County

"The last cattle drive the J. J. Cattle Company made; I rode the bell-horse to Dodge City, Kansas," Daddy told us. "I was happy with this chore as it was not dusty. The dust made riding the drag the least pleasant of all trail tasks."

"The bells were strapped around the neck of my horse. However, they were generally around the neck on a lead steer. I rode at the head of the procession. My horse was especially useful in starting a heard swimming across a river or getting the cattle to enter a pen. We lost cattle while crossing the Cimarron and Red River. At night, I muffled the bells or took them off so I wouldn't scare the cattle." Daddy never learned to swim.

"On that drive, I went to the chuck wagon for a meal. After ward, I became sick. I thought that it was because I was positive that the dishes had not been rinsed, and still had soap on them."

While the J. J. Cattle Ranch was a power in this country, there were quarrels between the J. J. cowboys and the sheepherders on the rangeland. The cowboys would chase the sheep, break up the flocks, rope the herders, and hurt many of them by dragging them with their lariats. After a quarrel, the cowboys issued an ultimatum, "Be gone with your sheep by sunup of a certain day or die. (22)

"By Gods, by sunup, --- (we) were hid in that dipping vat. Several cowboys showed up coming down a little canyon on their horses yelling and shooting their six guns. We didn't wait for them to get close until we answered theirs with our Winchesters. By the time we had killed some of the horses and wounded some of the men, they were ready to quit. They loaded the wounded behind them and rode out."

The range war between the cattlemen and sheepmen was finally over although there were still a few hard feelings left. Tommy did not like sheep. Therefore, he would not work on the McKenzie and McIntosh sheep ranches, which covered most of what is now Baca County, Colorado.

The Mexican people called the Las Animas River 'RIO DE LAS ANIMOS PERDIDAS IN PURGATORIO,' which means 'the river of lost souls in purgatory.'

Tommy did not pay much heed to the politics of the day when Woodrow Wilson was elected President of the United States in 1912.

The blizzard in the fall of 1912 saw deep snow that lasted through the winter. The J. J. lost cattle by the thousands. The J. J. went broke and a few years later went out of business.

Eastern Colorado was the land where, in 1868, Wild Bill Hickok, James Butler Hickok scouted General George W. Graham and Company I, of the Tenth Calvary. Near Kim, Wild Bill was wounded in his foot from a lance thrown by an Indian.

This country is where Clay Allison, the most feared gunfighter on the Western Frontier, killed Deputy Sheriff Charles Faber in a battle at the Olympia Dance Hall in Las Animas on December 21, 1876.

The story told was that 'Doc' John Henry Holliday DDS wounded a gambler named 'Kid' Colton in Trinidad, Colorado in 1879.

The same year 'Bat' William Barclay Masterson, who assisted Wyatt Earp in Tombstone, Arizona, traveled to Trinidad to bring the prisoner, 'Dutch' Henry Borne, back to Kansas for the trail.

Attracted by what he saw in Colorado, Masterson later came to Colorado to live. Another gambler and gunfighter, Ben Thompson visited Trinidad. Masterson said of Thompson, "It is very doubtful if in his time there was another man living who equaled him in a life and death struggle."

Barbed wire, the use of this new barrier sparked so-called Fence Wars between farmers-homesteaders and cattlemen. For many years, the ranchers annually had driven and grazed their cattle over the plains at will. Barbed Wire blocked the good grazing land and water holes. Violent disputes broke out throughout New Mexico, Texas, Wyoming, and other states such as Colorado. Native American called the wire "devils rope."

By 1914, fifty-three thousand claims for homesteads sprouted up throughout the Great Plains.

The Raper family moved near the settlement of Kim in eastern Colorado sometime before 1912 when Maud, Jacob's wife filed on a homestead.

I do not know why Jacob, my grandfather, was not the one to file on the land. The 1920 Census states that Jacob was 65 years-old and Maud was 40.

Jacob planned to build an outhouse, however in the meantime, the temporary potty was a hole in the ground some distance from the dugout. The hole had dirt piled up around it on three sides.

"What is that dang-hole doing out here?" One cowboy commented to his partner while they were riding nearby. "Who would dig such a thing anyway?"

"Darned if I know, a horse could break a leg in it, or we could have gotten throwed." Curiosity is getting the better of the two they rode closer and looked into the hole.

"Dad and I were out on the prairie," Daddy reciting the event to his children chuckled, "when we heard someone shrieking like a banshee."

"Of course', by the time we ran to see what was happening the cowboys had lit out of there like their tails were on fire. All we saw was their dust."

"Maud happened to be using the facility, with her skirts up when the men happened to ride by." A grin spread across Daddy's face at the memory. "You can bet we built an outhouse dam quick after that."

Jacob sat back opened the drawstring, poured a small amount of tobacco on the paper, licked the edge, rolled a cigarette and lit it. He picked up the weekly newspaper, the headline seemed to scream, **"Lusitania SUNK."**

Jacob continued to read. *The Lusitania (vessel) British steamship of the Cunard Line, torpedoed without warning by a German submarine, May 7, 1915, off the southern coast of Ireland. The ship sunk is less than 20 minutes with the loss of 1,198 persons including 128 Americans."*

"There is gonna be hell to pay," Jacob commented.

The Lusitania sank in less than 20 minutes with the loss of 1196 persons, including 128 Americans.

"What are you mumbling about," Maud asked.

"The Lusitania was sunk."

"What is a Lusitania?"

"It was a British ship."

The Germans asserted that the ship was carrying arms for the Allies (which later research proved factual) and that Americans was were warned against taking passage on British vessels in a notice that had appeared in American morning newspapers on the day the ship sailed from New York City. The unfairness of the German submarine warfare turned American public opinion against Germany. President sent several dispatches demanding that Germany make reparation. Germany refused.

One cold frosty morning in early 1917, Jacob was ill. "Son, will you go see Mr. --- up the canyon about some cattle for me?"

The fresh air felt good as Tommy was riding along, he started singing.

"If the ocean was whiskey and I was a duck, I'd dive to the bottom and never come up.

Rye Whiskey, Rye Whiskey, Rye Whiskey I cry, if you don't give me whiskey, I surely will die."

This song was the cowboys "hymn of praise" to the only friend who was guaranteed to give a warm greeting at the end of a long dusty trail.

It was late afternoon when he concluded his business with the man. As he rode out of the canyon onto the prairie, clouds were massing in ominous gray mounds with a yellowish tinge, a forewarning of a coming storm. His horse blew a cloud of misty breath into the cold air. Tommy urged his horse into a ground-eating lope.

Tommy's breath came out of his mouth in puffs of frozen air. Gusts of snow lashed at him. The moon shrouded in snow and there were no stars to guide the way. Tommy slowed his horse as he pushed his hat down further on his head, draped a wool scarf over his hat, and tied it under his chin to protect his ears from frostbite. The snow soon turned into an icy blizzard, which struck with astonishing fury obliterating everything. In the whiteout, Tommy could not see his hands in front of his face. The wicked winds dropped the temperature to well below freezing.

Blinded by the fury of the wind and the stinging snow he could not pick up the trail. The horse was having trouble making headway through the snow now chest high "top-wire'. The horse stumbled onto a fence line. The snowdrifts already choked with tumbleweeds, built up against the fences. A sense of desolation and helplessness came over the boy.

"Tony, blast you. Come On." Tommy uttered as he pulled on the reins to go the way he thought would lead him home. Tony did not agree.

"Well Tony, I reckon I'll stop fighting you. Maybe you have better sense then I do. So you head out." The scream of the wind swallowed the sound of his voice.

As he held tightly on to the saddle horn, his hands were freezing. Soon he was semi-conscious, lulled to sleep by the supernatural horse beneath him, whose hooves made a muffled whisper in the snow. They crossed over two fence lines on the frozen snow-packed drifts.

The stovepipe rattled as the scream of the wind threatened to funnel its full force directly down into the dugout, an odd noise caught Jacob's attention.

"Something's out there." The sound also caught Maud's attention. Jacob opened the door to investigate.

The horse whinnied, pawing the ground, blowing a cloud of breath into the cold air. Tommy's body slumped over the saddle, was barely visible in the wind and snow.

Maud battled to hold the door open against the wind, and the old man's arms trembled from the cold and strain as he lifted his son from the saddle and helped him into the dugout.

"Hope we don't have to amputate anything," Maud muttered as she scrapped a raw potato and applied the paste to the boy's nose, fingers, and toes to prevent frostbite.

"You ornery, mule-eared rascal, you saved my boy's life." Jacob talked to the horse while he rubbed the moisture from its coat, and checked its hooves and eyes.

"Here son," Jacob said lifting the boy's head, "drink some of this warm milk. Maud put a good dollop of whiskey in it. Drink it all. Now go to sleep." Jacob sat up all night by his son's side.

After the storm let up and Jacob deemed Tommy well enough to sit a horse, they went out to scout the area.

"Clear moon, frost soon," Jacob quoted," red sky at night, sheepherders delight, red sky in the morning, sheepherders take warning."

They found cattle that had drifted against the fence lines and had frozen to death where they stood. Occasionally, they spotted a vent hole with steam coming out of it, and then they would dig a live cow out. Jacob lost most of his cattle, as did many ranchers and farmers that winter.

The United States intercepted a note proposing a Mexican-German alliance. Germany promised Mexico the return of territory taken by the United States in the Mexican War between the years 1846-1848; the proposal would affect part of Colorado.

"We are declaring war on Germany," announced President Woodrow Wilson. ***"The world must be made safe for democracy."*** President Wilson claimed to be a great foe of imperialism, but no president meddled more in Latin American.

President Woodrow Wilson (1912 to 1919) led the United States during World War I. He claimed to be a great foe of imperialism, but no president meddled more in Latin America.

April 6, 1917, the United States declares war on Germany.

The United States joined France, Russia, Britain, and Italy to fight against their enemies (Central Powers) Germany, Austria, Hungary, and the Ottoman Empire (Turkey). Nationalism, imperialism, anti-colonial unrest, hostile alliance systems, militarism, and an army race were all the current problems.

The United States adopted the draft system for raising troops, and the first draft call came in July 1917. Colorado men soon were in almost every camp in the country. Many of the young men between the ages of 21 to 35 in the area marched to war.

The draft age limit of 21 to 35 liable for military service was later amended to require the 18 to 45 age group to serve their country.

"I received a summons to appear before a judge to explain why I had not responded to the draft notice," Daddy recalled. "I moved around working at the various ranches. It was over a month for the draft notice to catch up with me. The Judge knew me, or I could have ended up in jail."

In his later years, we children teased Daddy of being the first 'draft-dodger'.

"My friend, Frank Ogden and I joined up on May 25, 1918," Daddy recalled.

Britain wavered entering the war until German armies marched through neutral Belgium to attack France.

After the U. S. entered the war in April 1917, it rushed to raise and transport a military force known as the American Expeditionary Force, under the command of General John J. (Black Jack) Pershing.

The French and English needed the relief from the Americans, although the American forces were short of supplies, rations, equipment, trained soldiers, and ships to transport their troops. Therefore, pressed into service were cruise ships and seized German ships.

By June 1917 more than 175,000American troops were, training in France and one division was actually in the lines of the Allied sector near Belfort. By November 1918, the strength of the A.E.F. was nearly two million. From the spring of 1918, U.S. troops played an essential part in the fighting.

The First Division of the A.E.F. was one of the trained divisions and became one of the best in the world.

Tommy served with the American troops (A.E.F.) who were in the sector around Verdun. He served with the A.E.F. from October 17, 1918, to January 1919.

"Our troop first sailed to England where it continually rained. At last, Tommy saw England, however, not the way he originally planned with the 101 Wild West Show.

"You men quit standing around," ordered the Sergeant. "Get your butts in gear and pitch your tents on that hillside if you want to stay dry."

"We dug trenches around our tents so that the rain would drain away from the tents."

"What in the hell do those fellows think they are doing?" Frank asked Tommy and pointed to an English wagon. The drivers had hauled a wagonload of bread to the American soldiers.

"They had just dumped the unwrapped bread in the rain on the wet, muddy ground. We shook our fists, swearing at the drivers, exchanging hot words. Those damned English didn't like us much. We did not care for them."

"I didn't know that England would be such a wet, dirty country. The air felt like a cold, soggy blanket."

Frank and Tommy served together in the cold and mud of that miserable countryside, sometimes under fire, but always under orders. In the face of violent death, there is only the petrified and the insane. However, the lessons Tommy received in his life, and in the military, had given him a sense of duty and responsibility that was beyond fear.

In their tent at night, Tommy and Frank often talked of life, their families, their hopes, what they would do when and if they survived the horror of War. The two men's friendship lasted many years until he got word that Frank had died. Frank had a heart attack while in his outhouse near Howard, Colorado.

ARLENE JANOSKI

This was how my father must have felt while in battle:

I was a trembling, because I'd got to decide, forever, betwixt two things, and I knowed it. I studied a minute, sort of holding my breath, and then says to myself: "All right, then, I'll go to hell - !"

Excerpt from
The Adventures of Huckleberry Finn

The following statement pretty well sums up how most of the men felt about the government:

"Everybody says this here thing we're involved in ain't a war. Congress says it ain't a war. The President says it ain't a war. 'course the guys over here getting shot at say it's the best-dammed imitation thy ever saw." Mark Twain. Soldiers lived and fought in trenches that were miserable swamp-like holes in the ground. The channels were a perfect breeding ground for the diseases. There were lice on soiled clothes and bodies. There was also trench-foot when after the soldiers had stood in water for weeks at a time. Before the soldiers could bathe or wash their clothes, their socks would begin to grow to their feet.

The trenches cut through the battlefront that protected the troops from deadly artillery. The covered trenches provided a second line of defense in case enemies overran the firing lines, backed by machinegun fire, and the firing trenches. Each was about six to eight feet deep. Off-duty troops lived in dugouts in the support trenches. Supplies, food, and fresh troops moved to the front through a network of reserve and communication trenches which were a mire pit of mud when it rained.

Between the trenches of opposing forces lay No-Man's-Land. Crossing No-Man's-Land often resulted in death, because there was barbed wire and open to the sights of enemy guns.

"In France, I saw a horse injured in the battle shot and dumped into a lime pit. Its teammate broke loose and jumped into the lime pit too."

"One night Frank and I went into a little French town and drank a quantity of champagne. On the way back to camp, 'three-sheets to the wind,' we were signing 'Rye Whiskey, Rye Whiskey' not in tune but loud when we meandered through a Negro encampment."

Those fellows were not at all happy about our invasion.

They started chasing us while brandishing long knives. I swear those knives were three feet long. I didn't know what those fellows were yelling, but I certainly understood their meaning. Those knives were the motivation for us to run faster than we thought we could. We made a mad dash toward the sentry at the camp gate and ran right past him with champagne glasses and bottles intact."

"The French women were especially beautiful," he added with a smile while Mama glowered at him.

"I became acquainted with a man in camp. On visiting him in his tent, I was startled to see a certain photograph. The photograph had caught the image of a beautiful woman with a haunting sadness in her eyes. It was my mother."

"Hey, you dirty-livered, sneak-thief," I shouted and jerked the fellow to his feet. "What do you mean by stealing my photograph?"

"We cocked our fists. We presented our bloody noses to the Sergeant when he arrived."

"After calming down, we discovered that we each had a copy of the photograph. Indeed, we had the same mother. Walter Hall was my older half-brother. I wasn't aware that he even existed."

ARLENE JANOSKI

Walter Hall

Walter Hall was born June 3, 1883. Evidently, a previous marriage was not often the subject of discussion. The story told was that Josephine's parents had this first marriage annulled. They thought the man was a gambler.

The 1900 Census lists two grandchildren, Walter and Ida, in the home of Thomas G. Hall.

Daddy never saw Walter again as the troops deployed and the brothers lost touch with each other.

World War I was the first to see the use of gases as a weapon. The Germans made an all out attack using 'mustard gas.' The German chemist, Fritz Haber, directed the production of Mustard Gas. It proved more stable than chlorine gas and phosgene. Mustard gas could contaminate an area for days after its release. The Germans first used mustard gas in 1917.

The gas could cause irritated eyes, noses, throats, and lungs. It could cause death in minutes, by asphyxiation.

"Fall Back!" the sergeant ordered when the gas started flying. "Put on your masks."

Thousands of allied troops succumbed to the effects of gas, and because of the devastation, the gas became an instrument of psychological warfare as well as physical.

"The troops were all issued gas mask; which afforded some, but not complete protection. My gas mask proved to be faulty. I woke up in a cold storage unit where bodies were prepared for burial or sent home. Talk about one scared fellow. I was terrified of being buried alive as my mother had been."

Medical treatment at this time had not advanced in the fifty years since the Civil War. Many soldiers did not trust doctors. There were cases where men with wounds did not seek help until the sores festered and became gangrene or blood poisoning, many died as a result. However, more men died from diseases than from bullets. Many soldiers succumbed to influenza between 1917 and 1919.

> No Man's Land Lyrics –Eric Bogle – Album- Plain and Simple
> *Well how do you do, Private William McBride*
> *Do you mind if I sit here down by your graveside?*
> *A rest for a while in the warm summer sun*
> *I've been walking all day, and I'm done*
> *And I see by your gravestone that you were only 19*
> *When you joined the glorious fallen in 1916.*
> *Well I hope you died quick and I hope you died clean*
> *Or, William McBride, was it slow and obscene?*

The Germans formally surrendered, and signed an armistice, with the cease-fire going into effect at 11:00 a.m., November 11, 1918. War had been a costly one in lives lost and money spent. "My tour of duty was up. I came home on the R.M.S. Mauretania, the sister ship of the Lusitania." Great Britain requisitioned Cunard's prize liner, Mauretania, in 1914 to transport troops between England and the Mediterranean

"We hit a terrible storm as it plowed through the sea and several of the men were sick as we crossed the Atlantic. For a while, we thought our fate was going to be the same as the Lusitania."

"On the crossing, I thought of the war, and the months I spent in Europe. As we got closer to America, my thoughts raced ahead to home, and I wondered what awaited me there. When the ship finally docked, I was never more thankful than when I finally set my feet on dry ground. I vowed never to get these feet wet again."

"A ticker-tape parade was held for the returning soldiers in New York City. Frank and I had never seen such sights, and we did not know what to think as we marched through the streets. Bits of paper fell from the tall buildings covering us."

Tommy received his discharge on January 20, 1919, at Camp Owen Bierne, Texas. He would have been nineteen years old not twenty-four as stated in his papers. His enlistment papers reported that his occupation was a farmer, with brown eyes, black hair, and a dark complexion. It also said that he was five feet nine. He was close to six feet and weighed about 200 pounds in his later years.

At Fort Bliss, Texas for the 82nd Field Artillery were Curtiss JN-2 "Jenny's" airplanes. Their mission included scouting, observation, and courier service for the cavalry and infantry units on the ground.

Camp Owen Bierne was renamed Biggs Field in honor of Lt. James Berthes "Buster" Biggs who was killed in a plane crash October 27, 1918, at Beltran, France.

Note: The New York Public Library American History Desk Reference, page 149, states that approximately 43,000 Colorado men served their country in WWI, and of that number, 1,000 men were killed, and 1,759 were wounded.

The number of Americans serving in the war was 4,743,826. Battle deaths were 53,513, and other mortal causalities were 63,195. The direct cost of the war was 32.7 billion dollars.

I do not have a photo of my father in his World War I uniform; however the picture below is of my father-in-law, Joseph Charles Janoski. I imagine my father looked much the same.

7

ELSIE MAE SHAW
MY MOTHER

The name Oklahoma is the combination of two Choctaw words OKLA means 'people,' and HUMNMA means 'red.' "Indian Territory, a name given to the region of the United States west of the Mississippi River that the federal government set aside in the 19th century for occupation by relocated so-called civilized Native American tribes. It was part of the Louisiana Purchase. In 1834. The Purchase was ceded to five southeastern tribes diminished by the American Civil War, white settlement, and governmental non-tribal subdivision. In 1907, the last of the Indian Territory was incorporated into the Oklahoma territory."

Why and when our grandfather and grandmother, Theodore Shaw and Rosa Amanda Fansler, found themselves in this wild country I do not know. Theodore was born on February 25, 1870, in Indiana, his father Stephen was 27, and his mother Elsa (Fesler) was 19. They had 5 daughters and two sons.

George Fesle((a great-grandfather) a prominent farmer and stock-raiser of Kosciusko County, is a native of Pennsylvania, born in Cumberland County February 2, 1816, his parents, John and Rebecca (Rule) Fesler, being natives of the same State, and of German origin. When about a year old he was taken by his parents to Seneca County, New York, they locating on Cuyuga Lake, where they lived till our subject had reached his eleventh year. They then removed with their family to Seneca County, Ohio, returning to New York one year later, when they settled in Erie

County, on Eleven Mile Creek, the father dying in Erie County when our subject was in his thirteenth year. After the father's death the mother, with her family of six children, returned to Seneca County, Ohio, and shortly after removed to Norwalk, Huron County, Ohio, where George was apprenticed to learn the carpenter's trade, and for many years he followed that avocation. He was first married, in Ohio to Matilda Thorn, by whom he had four children- Sarah J., Abraham, Nancy A., and Rebecca, all of whom are deceased. In 1841 Mr. Fesler settled with his family in Whitley County, Indiana, remaining there till the fall of 1855. He then went to Minnesota, residing there some three years, and in the fall of 1858 he settled in Clay Township, Kosciusko County, Indiana, being among the pioneers of the county, and many were the hardships and privations he experienced in his pioneer home. His first wife died about eight years after marriage, and he was again married to Orilla Keeny, daughter of Rufus D. Kenny, who was formerly of Ohio, but at the time of her marriage lived in Noble County, Indiana. To this union were born four children – Elsie (Elsa), wife of Stephen Shaw of Kansas, John W., living in Marshall County, Indiana; Josephine, wife of John Kimmel of Dekalb County, Indiana, and George, living in Kosciusko County. In the fall of the same year of his return to Indiana (1858), he was again called to mourn the death of his faithful wife, who fell victim to typhoid fever, the then prevailing disease of the country. Mr. Fesler was a third time married, taking for his present wife Sarah Wyant, who was born in Champaign County, Ohio, in 1840, with her parents, Daniel and Ann Wyant, to Kosciusko County, Indiana, in 1852, where she has since lived. Five children have been born to this union – Mary, wife of John Dunn, of Jasper County, Indiana; Belle, wife of Charles Garrett; Charles, Alice, and Carrie, the last three living at home with their parents. In the wilds of Whitley, he began his first real life's work, clearing off the heavy forests, helping to raise the log cabins of his neighbors, and working at his trade, when work was to be had, in both Whitley and Kosciusko counties. The first good frame house in Washington Township he built for John Makemson, an old pioneer and his life-long friend. Here, while struggling against poverty and affliction, was formed of the great desire of his life: to obtain an education and join the active itinerancy of the Methodist Episcopal Church. But in this fate seemed to have reserved for his hand's other work. Licensed first as an exhorter, and then as a local preacher, he gave both of his time and means the best that he could to the support of the gospel, and, more than all, the record of an earnest Christian life and an upright manhood. He still lives, at the ripe age of seventy-one years, on a goodly heritage, the work of his own hands, surrounded by neighbors and friends whose confidence and esteem pay just tribute to his merit, and whose children will always say with pride, my father was George Fesler. (23)

Theodore's mother, Elsa/Elsie Fesler Shaw Jeffers passed away in 1929 in Horton, Kansas. She was 79 years old.

There was an economic crisis in 1893 while the family was living in Harper, Kansas.

At the age of 74, Grandpa Theodore Shaw died on April 19, 1944, due to an accident and is buried in Canon City, Colorado.

Rosa Fansler, our grandma, was born May 4, 1881, in Riley, Kansas.

Theodore and Rosa were married May 20, 1899, in Kay County, Oklahoma Territory.

My mother, Elsie Mae, began life on April 2, 1903, in Edith, Colorado. "The day I was born, so close to April fool's day," Mama once commented, "Daddy thought fate was playing a trick on him by giving him a girl instead of a boy."

"I was a namesake of my Grandmother, Elsie (Elsa) Fesler Shaw," mother recalled. "Grandma said that her husband, Steven, told her one day that he was going to the store to buy some tobacco. He walked down the railway track, and that was the last she ever saw of him. I guess he kept going and never looked back.'

In researching the family, I found that Steven Shaw returned to New York State where he lived with a son.

Exciting news also came in 1903 for in Kitty Hawk, North Carolina. Orville and Wilbur Wright made the world's first successful sustained human-crewed flights in a gasoline-powered aircraft. Wilbur stayed in the air 59 seconds, as his plane covered 852 feet.

"Well there are fools everywhere," Rosa commented about that event, "It's a wonder they didn't break their necks."

"Well, that's not all the news," Theodore told his wife. "Henry Ford has founded a company to make motor cars, and President Theodore

Roosevelt signed the legislation creating the National Wildlife Refuge System. Places where no one can hunt."

Mama was never sure whether she was born in Colorado or New Mexico. However, when she applied for Social Security, her mother and an uncle testified she had been born in the logging camp of Edith, Colorado, which borders New Mexico.

Edith, Colorado at an elevation of 7,082 feet was at one time a railroad terminus, and one of the most significant populated places in the area. It was unclear to some who had land claims in the area as to just where the state line was and several people were shot or killed over land disputes until federal surveyors established the line. Archuletta County named for J. M. Archuletta, a brother to a state senator, was one of the men killed in the disputes.

Edgar Biggs, owner of the large sawmill there, named the town Edith in honor of his daughter.

Loggers lived in camp throughout the year. They labored all day, endured extreme weather, and worked among life-threatening conditions. A particularly dangerous occupation was that of the river drivers. To get the logs to the mill these fearless men walked on the rolling logs floating downstream. The harshness of the occupation and the hardness of the men inspired many stories and songs. In American folklore, loggers were romanticized as legendary characters such as the powerful Paul Bunyan and Blue, his great ox.

Construction of Rio Grande Southern, in 1891 formed a vast arc of 3 ft. Narrow gauge trackage through the densely forested regions in the La Plata and San Miguel Mountain ranges. Most of the RGS's equipment old and used second-hand or more ancient, locomotives. There were 162 miles of rail trackage through the rugged terrain of the Rocky Mountains between Durango and Ridgeway.

In 1901 and 1902, with available railroad facilities for his logging interests in the town of Dolores Biggs bought cutting right in large stands of timber north of that town.

Logging in the Edith region had stripped much of the available timber. Which, in 1914, the New Mexico Lumber company was forced to pull its operations back into New Mexico.

At the present day, Edith is now a bridge across the Navajo river with a couple of houses and is a ranching community to mark the area that was once Edith.

After Mama's death in 1986, I discovered that a file existed in the Edith records for Elsie Mae Shaw in box 4, docket 306. She was indeed born in Edith, Colorado,

One night, Theodore and Rosa were walking home after attending a party at the logging camp. He was carrying his baby daughter. As they were crossing over a railroad bridge, Theodore felt the back of his neck prickling. He looked around but could see nothing in the darkness gathering around them. Something was out there following them. He picked up the pace and started walking faster and faster; it was no longer a leisurely stroll home.

"Shaw! Slow down." Rosa fussed at her husband; Rosa never called her husband by his first name. He did not slow his pace making it difficult for his wife to keep up. Rosa had spinal meningitis as a child and as a result; she had a limp, which plagued her all her life.

Rosa grabbed her husband's coattail and held on all the way home where he hurried her into the house.

"Shaw, let the dog in." Teddy, their terrier, was whimpering at the door. Theodore ignored his wife while locking the door and checking the windows. Outside, Teddy's hackles rose and quickly found a hole under the house.

Just at that moment, Rosa jumped when she heard a shriek. "That's a woman," she whispered, "a woman screaming."

"No, that was a big cat. I remember hearing a tale told that there was a man attacked by a grizzly when a Mountain Lion defended him. I heard a cat once conversing with its mate. It was cooing like a pigeon. Sometimes the cats sob like a woman, emitting a slight flat shriek as we heard."

Rosa paced the floor all that long, dark, night. However, the baby slept peacefully.

In the morning, Theodore informed his wife that he was going outside after breakfast.

"Shaw isn't that dangerous," Rosa remarked as she turned the flapjacks. "That cat could still be out there."

"It is most likely back in the hills by now," he said sipping his coffee. "Cats usually stay in their territory up in the rough country. They can hiss, issue a bubbling growl, or mew like a kitten. The cat ranges as much as twenty-five miles wide, and their hunting ground is shrinking because so many people are moving in and taking over their territory."

As Theodore pushed his plate away, he continued, "Some Indians in this area consider the meat of a Mountain Lion a delicacy. They also draw their origins at the Creation of ancestral mountain lions as well as bears."

While Theodore investigated, Teddy sniffed the paw prints in the snow where the mountain lion had evidently followed them home the night before.

"You are one lucky dog, Teddy, that cat must have thought you would make a good meal."

The puma or mountain lion (Felis Concolor) is the most significant member of the cat family in North America. Puma's are solitary animals. Because of the cats' limited contact, fighting between pumas rarely occur. The hunting territories for the adult cat overlaps less than those of other cats do, even though the migration pattern of their primary prey, mule deer, and elk, reduce productive hunting grounds during the winter. The cats will also eat porcupines, even grasshoppers on occasion.

Theodore and a few of the men from camp, with the help of dogs, tracked the lion up into the hills. They finally treed the cat. The cat's nervous tail flicked back and forth, as its yellow eyes watched every move the men and dogs made. However, none of the men was brave enough to approach too closely.

"You can bet we all jumped when that cat snarled with such ferocity at us," Theodore recalled.

One of the men tried to throw a rope over the cat's head, but the cat just batted it away. Then the cat made a mighty leap and was gone before the men could raise their guns to shoot.

"Biggest cat I ever heard the tale of." Hank, with his wild red hair standing on end, spread his hands wide apart; to show how enormous were the paws of the cat.

"With each new telling," Theodore chuckled, "the cat just grew larger and larger."

After moving to Oklahoma, Theodore was working several miles from his home when he noticed a narrow rotating column in the sky with an intense vortex. At home, Rosa also saw the air and ran with her daughter to a neighbor's storm cellar. The little girl's eyes were round with fear. "Daddy, I want my Daddy."

The tornado plucked trees, animals, and people from the ground throwing them like matchsticks. Some buildings had exploded because the pressure inside was much more significant than outside.

A neighbor found his Granny lying peacefully on her bed, and the covers on the bed were not even rumpled. "I knew the good Lord would take care of me," was Granny's explanation.

People call this area 'Tornado Alley.' The tornadoes are most common here in April, May, and June.

During his life, Theodore had acquired sufficient education to qualify as a schoolteacher. However, he preferred not to pursue this line of work. Theodore could turn his hand to many trades; nevertheless, my grandfather chose to be a plaster and stonemason. He followed that profession to Texas.

Among the friends that six-year-old Elsie made in Texas was an attractive Indian woman who sold beaded necklaces and moccasins.

"I especially admired one necklace made with dried cherry seeds interspersed with blue seed beads." The woman thought the little girl was charming with the big blue eyes. She gave her the necklace.

Mama treasured that necklace all her life, and I have cherished it since my mother's death.

"Meow?" the big gray cat questioned. "Meow?"

"Now, don't you know that isn't so," Mrs. D answered the cat. Mrs. D often conversed with the cat as she moved around the house. They seemed to understand each other very well. Mrs. D ran the boarding house where the Shaw's were staying.

Fascinated, Elsie sat down on a step to watch. The cat greeted her, purring and rubbing against her ankles.

"What is your kitty's name?" Elsie asked.

"My 'Grimalkin'?" The woman asked turning to face the little girl. "Why that is Mr. D. of course." The word grimalkin usually denotes an old gray female cat or a shrewish old woman, but it made no difference to Mrs. D. She loved that old cat.

"Grimalkin, you know, is the reincarnation of my late husband. That is why I call him Mr. D.

"A re-in-in-in?" The little girl stammered.

"You see, my husband was reborn or reincarnated in the body of my 'Grimalkin.'"

The little girl was confused all the more. How could a big man fit into the body of a cat?

Mrs. D sat a dish of milk on the floor for the cat. Satisfied, the cat strolled off down the hall, gracefully waving his tail, a white beard of fluid hanging from his chin.

Later that day Elsie asked, "Mama what is re-in-car-nation?"

"Where did you hear that nonsense?"

"Mrs. D said ---."

"Pay no heed to the ramblings of that demented woman."

"What is de-men-ted?"

"Never you mind. Go out and play."

One night Rosa nudged her tired husband. "Shaw these partition walls don't go all the way to the ceiling. I can hear everything that is said and done in the other rooms."

"Uh," he moaned and turned over on his side.

The little girl lying in her bed looked up at the ceiling and saw that what her mother was saying was true. The walls missed meeting the roof by about two feet.

Rosa accosted Mrs. D the next day in the hallway, "Mrs. D, the noise and strange smells in this house is very annoying. Why don't the walls meet the ceiling?"

"Well," Mrs. D--- huffed at Rosa for daring to question her. "The walls happened to be built that way for the heat to circulate in the winter."

"Top of the morning to ye." The housekeeper interrupted them.

One day Elsie was sitting on the top step watching the Irish woman on her hands and knees scrubbing the floor. The two had gotten to be quite friendly. The little girl was fast picking up the woman's brogue and could imitate her quite well.

"Why don't the walls go all the way up to the ceiling?" Elsie shot questions at the woman. "What is that strange smell? Is it perfume? Mama doesn't wear perfume."

"Now you never mind, Missy." The woman laughed waving off further questions with a wet rag. "Go on outside and play, why don't ye."

"Shaw, we are going to have to move." Rosa was still complaining about the noise and smell in the boarding house. "I cannot stand it a minute longer."

A commotion stirred at the boarding house one day when police arrested a Chinaman who lived in one of the rooms. He had been smoking opium. That settled the question of the strange smell.

"I always believed," Mama once told me, "the Irish housekeeper was an undercover agent because she disappeared the same day they took that Chinaman away."

"After roller-skating all one day I woke up the next morning shaking with the chills. I had a fever, sore throat, headache, and a cough." Influenza had come to town, and many people were ill.

"I was well, and ready to go skating. However, Mama had other notions and never let me go skating again. She thought that was what caused me to get sick, especially when she found I had been skating in the rain."

"I was pretty downhearted about my skates when I heard the Captain."

"Here girl," the old Captain commanded, "don't you be running out in the rain again."

The old sailor was also staying at the boarding house. In the parlor, he had regaled the blue-eyed girl with many of his high sea adventures.

She liked the old man with his Captain's cap perched on his bald pate and his gap-tooth smile wide in his grizzled beard. There were squint lines about his twinkling eyes from years of sun, wind, and exposure from his many years at sea.

"Don't you have a Nor'easter?"

"I don't think so. What is a Nor'easter?"

"Trim your sails a minute, and I will be right back."

The Captain returned with a present. It was a Nor'easter. A yellow raincoat.

"This will keep you high and dry."

As she put on the coat, he commented, "You look like a little yellow bird."

"*Goodbye, Little Yellow Bird,*" the Captain sang. Yellow Bird was a favorite song of the time.

"*I love you little yellow bird, but I love my freedom too, so goodbye little yellow bird, I'd rather brave the cold, on a leafless tree, than a prisoner is, in a cage of gold."*

"Oh, thank you. It is the best present I ever received," Elsie whispered and kissed the old man's cheek.

"One day, Mama and I were standing in front of the general store, when suddenly she hustled me inside the store."

"I wondered why Mama seemed so frightened. I peeked around her skirts and looked out the window. A man is walking up the street. He had a mustache and was dressed in a black suit and hat. He had a pistol, strapped to his hip."

While the little girl was examining the man with unblinking scrutiny, the man suddenly seemed to feel her stare. He looked up at her and smiled. "It was a nice smile. I did not understand Mama's fear."

"I heard Mama later that day," Elsie recalled, "relating the scene to Daddy.

"That man was a gunfighter," Rosa told her husband." I just know it."

"Why, the way you describe him, it sounds like Clyde Maddox," Theodore told her. "The description fits. I have seen him about town a time or two."

Note: I have yet to find a gunfighter by that name in any of the books I have read. The only name that e close was Chris Madson born in 1844

"Not many days after this incident, I saw a man leaning against a post. When Mama and I came near, he stooped down to pick me up. I started screaming and kicking."

"Elsie, what on earth is the matter with you?" her mother scolded, "Don't you recognize your own Daddy?"

Finally, through her tears, as he talked to her, the little girl realized it was indeed her Daddy; but he had shaved off his mustache.

Wiping the tears from his daughters face he said, "I promise, baby, that I will never shave my mustache again." Moreover, he kept that promise for the rest of his life.

"The dress I wore on my first day at school," Elsie recalled, "Mama had cut down from one of her dresses. At recess, the girls were jumping rope or tossing a ball to one another. On the other side of the schoolyard, the boys were choosing teams to play baseball. I thought it would be more fun with the boys than jumping rope, so I crossed the yard to watch. I did not know that the teacher had expressly forbidden the girls to cross the centerline of the schoolyard. So I was in serious trouble.

"The girl's outhouse was a two-holer. The boy's outhouse was across the schoolyard. The boys would throw rocks at the girl's outhouse when the teacher was not looking. One day a girl started screaming. William had thrown a red-racer (snake) through the hole in the back of the outhouse. From then on one girl would stand guard when another girl was using the facility. It was cold that winter, it always took me several minutes to unbutton my all clothes and hike up my skirt. I would not sit on the wooden seat. I was afraid my bottom would freeze."

"If the teacher caught the boys making some mischief she punished them by making them chop wood, carry it into the schoolhouse. They also carried water from the well, or shovel snow." "Class dismissed." The teacher rang the little bell that sat on her desk.

"Elsie you remained seated."

"A few girls cast sideways glances at me. Some gave me a look of sympathy. The boys only snickered but greatly relieved that they were not the victim of their stern teacher."

"But Mama is ---," Elsie tried to explain that her mother was sick at home and had told her to come home immediately after school.

"Young lady!" The teacher gave Elsie a 'Keep Your Mouth Shut' look. "There will be no excuses. Your mind was wondering. You failed to know that Arizona and New Mexico became the forty-seventh and forty-eighth states of the Union. You will write Arizona and New Mexico each one hundred times on your slate."

"Shaw!" In the meantime, Rosa was calling her husband, and she was angry. "Shaw, I told Elsie to come straight home. That lazy girl must be doddering somewhere."

"Go find her!" Rosa demanded. "She has chores to do."

Removing his hat as he stepped inside the weather-beaten schoolhouse door. Suddenly the strident voice of the teacher was heard berating his daughter. He was a man who seldom showed anger, but now a spasm of irritation crossed his face.

"Mr. Shaw ---," the teacher flinched when she noticed him. "Elsie is being disciplined because of---." She closed her mouth when she saw his eyes blazing like blue stars. A muscle was twitching in his jaw. Theodore never uttered a word but motioned his daughter to him. They turned and left the building.

"Daddy seldom showed anger and would never say a bad word against anyone. The most he ever said in the way of criticism was, 'They'll do to let alone.'"

"I don't know if anything was later said to the teacher," My mother recalled. "But she never kept me after school again."

Theodore held his daughter's hand as they strolled toward home. The graceful prairie grasses undulated in the gentle breeze, and the wildflowers nodded in the late afternoon warmth.

"Pit, Pit, Pit!" Elsie turned toward the sound. "Pit, pit."

"Ha, ha, ha!" She laughed. "Look, Daddy." A little upright Quail with a waving topknot, which looked like a woman's Sunday bonnet, strolled across the path. Ten babies, in a straight line, played follow-the-leader behind their mother.

A quiet chuckle made his thick mustache twitch. The quail reminded him of the huffing teacher. Watching his daughter, he was pleased that the encounter with her teacher and the inevitable confrontation with her mother were in the far recesses of her mind for the moment. Theodore lifted up his tired little girl carrying her the last mile. Elsie felt safe in the arms of her father. He had taught her today that she was loved.

Twilight found them entering the house. Rosa looked at them. An angry hot flush burned her cheeks. "Shaw, where have ---?"

"Hush." Theodore silenced his wife then put his sleepy little daughter to bed.

I believe Grandpa Shaw moved his family back to Colorado sometime in 1910 or earlier.

A swirling funnel hanging from a dark cloud mass was coming out of the southwest. Theodore threw down his tools and ran home. He was, relieved to find his wife and nine-year-old daughter unharmed who had taken shelter in the root cellar.

"After the storm," Elsie recalled, "we found straws driven through trees. I even saw a cow lodged in the upper branches of a tree. Family photographs were found several miles away."

Early settlers planted wheat in 1914-1915, and their yield was 60 bushels to the acre. D. O. Simpson established a post office, and store on a corner of his homestead, in the South Eastern plains of Colorado, March 1917.

Rudyard Kipling's novel, 'Kim' was immensely popular at the time. December 8, 1918, the community chose the name of Kim, in honor of 'Kipling's' boy hero. Mrs. Lula Jeffries became the postmistress.

The little-isolated town of Kim was born. Located in the southeastern part of Las Animas County, Colorado at an elevation of 5,690 feet and situated on a high divide, which divides the waters of the Canadian and Arkansas Rivers.

Wilma Good wrote:

"As near as I have been able to ascertain the first restaurant was in Old Kim and was run by some people by the name of Shaw. Old Kim lay north and adjacent to the original U.S. No. 160 Highway, which went east from the north side of the cemetery and continued east and south until it came out about 2 or 3 miles north of Campo onto what is now Highway 287."

Theodore chose the corner of Main and (Las) Animas Streets to build a rock hotel or Halfway House that had three or more bedrooms. Rosa cooked and served family style meals. There was one permanent roomer, Mr. Mosley, a carpenter. Both Mr. Rowland and Theodore operated the hotel. S. J. Matthew established a general store, and in 1920, Dickey's General Merchandise came to town.

Newspapers called these eastern plains of Colorado, 'The Great American Desert'. Referred to as 'The High Plains,' is the arid region of North America. Good farmland and ranch land enticed settlers to homestead in the area. In the 1920's, a population explosion happened. These people had the spirit of adventure, bravery, and resourcefulness. Most of the land-hungry homesteaders built sod houses, board shanties, of dugouts. While the farmers tilled under the buffalo and Gamagrass, cattle were grazing the open range which had been pastureland for the vast herds of buffalo.

When the Surveyors marked the boundaries of the homesteads, they used a well, or a house as a starting point, sometimes even a plowed field. The surveyors used a hundred foot rope or counted the revolutions of a wheel to mark the distance around the tracts making the road jag around them making right angle turns.

Orson Pratt, a Mormon pioneer, recorded in his journal the details regarding his ingenious "double endless screw."

"For several days Mr. Clayton (ED.: the camp historian) and several others have been thinking about the best method of attaching some machinery to a wagon, to indicate the number of miles daily traveled. I was requested this forenoon by Mr. B. (Brigham) Young to give the project some attention; accordingly, this afternoon I proposed the following method: — Let a wagon wheel be of such a circumference that 360 revolutions be one mile. . . Let this wheel act upon a screw in such a manner that six revolutions of the wagon wheel shall give the screw one revolution. Let the threads of the screw act upon a wheel of sixty cogs, which will evidently perform one revolution per mile. Let this wheel of sixty cogs be the head of another screw, action upon another wheel of thirty cogs; it is evident that in the movements of this second wheel, each cog will represent one mile. Now if the cogs are numbered from 0 to 30, the number of miles traveled will be indicated during every part of the day. Let every sixth cog of the wheel be numbered 0 to 10, and the division will indicate the fractional part of a mile or tenths; while if anyone should be desirous to ascertain still smaller divisional fractions, each cog between the divisions will give five and one-third rods. This machinery (which may be called the endless double screw) will be simple in its construction and of very small bulk, requiring scarcely any sensible additional power . . . the weight of this machinery need not exceed three pounds."

The odometer, as constructed by a skilled mechanic according to Pratt's instruction, cut in the middle of wind-swept Wyoming, was small enough to be contained in a box 18 inches long, 15 inches high and three inches thick. The original model is in the Deseret Museum at Salt Lake City, Utah.

"We had no radios, television, airplanes, modern plumbing, heating or cooling, few automobiles, no graded roads, culverts, or bridges in the country of Kim, Colorado."

This land is where the Purgatoire, or the 'Picketwire,' as the old-timers call it, flows between banks of brown and tan soil to join the Arkansas River.

Rosa's brother, John Roger Fansler and his wife, Mary, died leaving five children: Martha, Charles Peter, Helen and the twins Earl and Carl. The children came to stay with their Aunt Rosa and Uncle Theo.

"Mama, please don't let Martha and Helen play with my doll," Elsie begged. "They will break it." I always kept it wrapped and safe when I was not playing with it. Now it was in Mama's hands ready to give to Martha and Helen.

It was a shock to the young girl to share everything with the girls. She did not want to share her doll that her Daddy had given her last Christmas.

"Shame on you," Rosa chastised her daughter. "Let the girls play with it. After all, they have lost their mother. It is the least you can do."

"Martha, you always get what you want," Elsie cried. "You are too prissy, afraid to get your hands dirty." She stuck out her tongue at Martha. Before her mother could catch her, she ran to the barn. At that moment, Elsie hated her cousins and vowed revenge.

One day the five children left to live with another relative.

Elsie later found her baby doll with its face cracked and the dress and torn and muddy. She did not get revenge as the cousins soon returned to their home.

When Elsie was fifteen, Martha, the dreaded cousin, came to revisit her Aunt Rosa again.

"Elsie," her mother called. "I need you to go gather cow chips. Take Martha with you." Cow chips, dried cow manure, were used to burn in place of the scare firewood or coal. Ten to twelve bushels of this 'surface coal' had to be gathered and stored against the coming winter.

"This chore is demeaning," Martha, a year or so older retorted to the request, but Rosa was unrelenting. Martha disliked getting her hand dirty and donned a pair of gloves.

At times, the overpowering aroma was as bad as the fresh dung in the barn. The only good part of the task was being out on the open prairie and seeing all the wildflowers blooming.

The girls were busy with their heads down gathering the chips; they did not see the wild-eyed demon staring at them.

The bull cocked his massive head and followed the fluttering skirts of the girls with beady eyes. He snorted, pawed the ground and tossed his great horns in the air.

Elsie turning toward the snorting bull screamed, "Run, Martha! Run." But there was no place to hide in this flat, treeless grassland. Not even a buffalo wallow.

Martha shrieked and looked about wildly.

Suddenly, a lariat snaked out catching the bull's right fore-hoof and both hind hooves, throwing the 700-pound to the ground within a few feet of the girls.

The man on horseback rewarded the frightened girls with a grin. His wide-brimmed hat low on his forehead and a five o'clock shadow graced his face. He led the bull off a good distance turning him loose. Touching the brim of his Stetson in a salute to the girls, he rode away. Nevertheless, the girl with pigtails and eyes the hue of the clear blue sky stayed in the mind of the young man. This cowboy was to become her husband.

Theodore, Rosa and Elsie.

Elsie Mae Shaw

8

SOD BUSTERS

Excerpt from my mother's Journal:

"Some of the first settlers around Kim, Colorado in 1918 were a family by the name of Jake Thompson. He started a garage and a man by the mane of Simpson that had a little store, and Post Office in a dugout a mile distance from where Kim is now. Then a family came and started a restaurant by the name of Euing (sic). The wife's name was Golda. I worked for them for three weeks for three dollars a week. Clarence insisted that I quit. My folks, Theo Shaw, bought Euings out. Then they decided to move Kim one mile south of the present location. There was two doctor's there in 1919, a Dr. G. W. Seay and Dr. Harvey K. Hill. (Dr. Hill delivered Elsie's first two children.) Father helped build the bank building then he built a rock boarding house. A Mrs. Jeffers ran the Post Office in 1920. Ortho la Rue had a rooming house."

The Shaw family was expecting Clarence at any moment. He had recently been discharged from the army. "His family and friends seldom called him Tommy, however, I always called him Clarence," Mama said.

"I was very nervous," Mama said. "I wanted to look my very best when he saw me." She was ready to comb out her braids went her mother's voice jarred her from her reverie.

"Elsie," her mother called, "the cow needs milking.

'I did 't take time to change back into my work dress." Leaving her hair in braids, Elsie ran to the barn.

"It will only take a few minutes to milk the cow and feed her," she thought. She sat down on the little three-legged stool and began to milk her." Bessie, a most docile cow, sensed the nervousness in the girl's hands, moved her rump and bumped into the girl.

"The milk pail went one way, and I ended up sprawled on the ground in a pile of fresh manure," mother recalled. "Oh no! My dress! Look at what you did," she shouted at Bessie.

Her blue eyes glistened with angry tears. Her braids, the color of golden wheat, had dirt and straw on them.

At that inopportune moment the tall, darkly handsome man walked into the barn.

"I fell in love with her," Daddy told us. "I began courting her in earnest that day."

That day Clarence sang on the way home: *"Good-by, old trail boss, I wish you no harm; I'm quitting this business to go on a farm. I'll sell my old saddle and buy me a plow; and never, no never, will I rope another cow."*

Daddy purchased a team of mules from the 101 Ranch and helped Theodore during the hay season or plowed a field.

Mr. Shaw and Clarence got along very well, and Theodore thought of him as the son he never had. However, Rosa was another matter. The big German woman did not hide her prejudice toward him.

"April 10, 1919, just eight days after my sixteenth birthday," Mama recalled, "Mr. Moulton, lost two of his sons, 14 and 15 years old."

The Moulton boys had been walking home when they reached Mr. Brenner's farm. It was getting quite late. Mr. Brenner invited them to stay the night. The boys decided that since they were only 10 miles from home, they could make it in no time. A blizzard came that night and was still raging the next morning. After the storm, neighbors found the boys frozen to death in a snowdrift.

"April 11, 1919," Daddy recalled, "I woke up that morning built a fire in the stove. Outside the powdery snow was blowing violently. I could not see the barn from the house. I had to feed the animals, so I tied a rope to a post by the house. Hanging onto the rope, I fought my way to the barn where I tied the rope to the barn door. When I finished my chores, I stepped back into the blizzard. I couldn't see my hand in front of my face. The cold air made catch my breath and cough. If I had lost my grip on that rope, I don't think I would have found my way back to the house."

"I was working taking care of the storekeepers' baby earning three dollars a month," Elsie said. "I was saving my money, but Mama would usually give me a list of things to buy to bring home. One time, I saved enough to buy a skirt."

"That skirt is too gaudy," Rosa declared. "No daughter of mine would wear such a thing."

"I was angry when Elsie told me about the confrontation with her mother." Daddy could not stand the way Mama's mother treated her. "I talked the matter over with Mr. Shaw and asked his consent to an early marriage."

The sun was coming up; it was going to be a beautiful spring day. Elsie was up at dawn getting her few belongings together. Feeling warm and giddy with anticipation she twirled around in her small bedroom. She brushed through her long, thick, hair until it shined like spun honey. She went to the well to get fresh water and twirled around and around with the bucket of water.

"**This is the day that I will be married,**" Elsie shouted to the bluebirds flying overhead. "**I will be Mrs. Clarence Thomas Rapier.**"

"Elsie," Rosa jarred her daughter back to reality, "there are chores to do."

Daddy drove in the yard. It would be a long trip to Springfield, the county seat, and he was anxious to get started.

"Daddy could not go with us," Mama told me. "He couldn't leave the animals that long." Rosa had insisted on accompanying the young couple. She was not about to let her daughter be unchaperoned with this man, this wild cowboy. She was hoping that her daughter would change her mind. After helping Rosa into the wagon seat, Theodore waved them off.

"May 6, 1919, Know by all men by these present that Clarence Rapier and Elsie Shaw," the Justice of the Peace with great deliberation said, "personally appeared before me.'

"You promise," The Reverend looked up sternly at the young people, "that from now on you will love, honor each other, for better or worse. Herein, fail not, so help you, God."

Clarence helped his young bride onto the wagon seat, relegating his mother-in-law to the back of the wagon despite protests and grumbling. Clarence tucked the horse's reins between his knees, turned to give his wife her first hug and kiss. He snapped the reins to hurry the horses a little faster and grinned to himself as the wheels of the wagon stirred up a small cloud of dust and seemed to hit every rock and hole. Rosa tumbled back on the blankets. He hardly noticed when the evening sun was lowering on the horizon. Sprinkles of rain came to quince the thirsty land.

To prove up a homestead a person had to show improvements, keep at least 40 acres in cultivation and have continuous residence six months each year for three years within a five year period. The law modified to accommodate the settlers during World War I.

There were no trees on the prairie. It was many miles to the mountains to cut trees. So without trees to build with, homesteaders had to rely on the only available material—prairie sod. Sod is the top layer of earth that includes grass with the dirt clinging to the roots.

Note: Our Story American History stories and Activities You Can Do Together. Historic Time Period: 1801-1861.

Choosing the right location for a homestead was very important. Looking for land which featured a stream or a creek was difficult for there were few on the prairie, so they searched for the possibility of a productive well.

"Why are you doing that?" the curious girl asked her husband as she watched him draw a line in the dirt one evening.

"I want to line up with the North Star. It will be the mark to start the north wall from." He answered. The next morning he dug a ten by twelve-foot hole in the ground four feet deep.

Cutting turf was a difficult task. Daddy then chose an area were the virgin prairie grass was the thickest and the most durable. He did not have a tractor with a plow equipped with curved steel blades to cut through the tough roots of the sod. So he used his horses. He was advised not to cut more grass than he planned to use in one day as the sod quickly dried, cracked, and crumbled if not used immediately. The sod bricks were 12 inches by 24 inches.

Most of the 'Soddies' were 16 by 24 feet, but my mother told me that theirs was only 10 by 12 feet. Freshly cut sod bricks weighed about 50 pounds each. They were laid root side up for the roots to continue to grow into the block above it. Over time, the blocks grew together to form a study wall.

The horses strained to pull the plow, turning over the furrows of sod that revealed fertile earth, which was the right width and depth that he needed. He cut the turf in three feet long pieces. He stacked them on a float which was made of planks and drove the team back to the building site.

Windows were expensive, so he left open areas for a door and one window. He set the frame into the wall then laid cedar poles over the gaps. Any spaces left were stuffed with rags to protect the windows from breaking and keep the cold wind out.

Daddy laid cedar poles across the sod walls. Tar paper was the next layer, then sod, grass side down was put on top of the poles to make a roof. He installed a stove pipe through the sod. While Daddy was building the walls, Mama's job was to apply clay mulch to the cracks in the walls and around the windows.

Their home was a one-room dugout built in the side of a small hill. Half of it was in the ground. The upper half was sod. This is called a half-Soddy. A hovel built from overturned sod.

This was an irritation to Elsie as it was dirty when the dust blew and leaky when it rained. Newspapers or sheets, or tar paper were nailed to the walls and ceiling. This was to try to keep the dirt from falling and the mice from entering, or an occasional snake from falling into the house.

This Soddy was Daddy and Mama's first home, and they were as proud of it as if it were a mansion.

Excerpt from Elsie's journal:

"We had a bed, a stove, and two boxes to sit on, and an apple box that served as our table. Flour sack or greased paper was put in the window until glass could be ordered."

Good old-fashioned sweat was about all it cost to build. The Soddy stayed cool in the summer and warm in the winter. One drawback was that the small window did not allow much light to penetrate the interior. The Soddy had poor ventilation. Little sod houses dotted the prairie like sentinels of safety to any lonely traveler.

Daddy applied a lesson that he learned in the Army by digging a trench around the house to keep the rain from running into the house.

Excerpt from Elsie's journal:

"There was no insulation, so we used feed sacks or newspaper tacked to the wall to keep the dirt from sifting down. The Soddy was low to the ground so that there was no fear of wind causing damage. We also felt safe should a tornado come for it was safe as a storm cellar".

"Our place was ten miles south of Kim. The Mesa View School was on the northwest corner of the place. Some of our neighbors were Josie and Jessie Howard, a schoolteacher at Meadie Veld (sic, Frank James, he was the brother of Jessie James, and Charles Carter was a brother-in-law to the Brites (sic). There was Balley's (sic), McLaghting (sic). Mrs. McLaghting was setting on Jake Thompson home with their small boys."

"The Bill Randell's (sic) lived one mile north of my folk's place. Mr. and Mrs. Lang (sic) Fletch (sic), Williams bought Rev. Talley's place was north of Daddy's place. Axtell's (sic) was east. Lee Axtell was convicted and sent to Canon City (state prison) for killing the Post Office Master."

"There was s a family, Lee Martize (sic) that owned the Pine Springs. Then on up the canyon was Noah Bishop. He lost a lot of cattle, as well as so many of the homesteaders on April 8, 1919 when the blizzard hit at six in the morning." There was also an Ed Ogden."

"The Rapier's lost the milk cow. My folks did not lose any of their stock because my father had built a good shelter under a hill. There were good corrals and plenty of feed. It stormed for three days. All creeks and draws were snowed full."

"Shaw, the eggs are disappearing. Could be it a fox?" Rosa queried holding a spoon up with batter on it. "I don't have enough to finish this cake."

"Well, when I heard about the eggs I knew I was caught red-handed," Daddy said, "and on my way to the dog house. That woman could sure get her dander up."

"I was doing what he had always done; feed the eggs to the horses to make their coats shiny and slick." He had learned this when he was a young boy tending his father's horses. He also gave the horses Garrett Snuff to kill the botfly worms.

"One day, I noticed that the horses would not eat their grain. They seemed to be frightened and stamping their feet. I opened the grain box and discovered a bull snake in it. I hate snakes. I killed it."

"Clarence," Mr. Shaw told me, "I wish you had not done that." He had even named the snake Teddy. That old bull snake killed rattlesnakes, rats, and mice in the barn."

A woman's first big task was to turn whatever awaited her arrival into a home, which was no small achievement. The living quarters ranged from the dirty, leaky, mud-brick 'Soddy' cabins to cave like dugouts built into the sides of hills, at their most sophisticated, one room, and dirt-floor log cabins.

Elsie, a sixteen-year-old girl, learned at an early age to cook and care for the family. The chores of the young wife were preparing the meals, (remember there was no electricity or refrigerators), sewing, milking the cow, tending the chickens, taking care of various cuts and wounds her husband received. She also helped butcher the animals. She made lye soap. Occasionally, she found time to do fancy work such as piecing a quilt, crocheting, tatting, knitting, or found a few moments to read. The insufficient light from the kerosene lamp made it difficult to see, so at times she took her tasks out into the sunshine. Trimming the wick and cleaning the chimney was essential. She sprinkled the dishwater on the dirt floor then would sweep it to make a hard surface.

Excerpt from my mother's journal:

"Free-ranging cattle were allowed to roam the countryside without restraint. Occasionally one of the cows would find its way on top of our house dirt would fall inside then. I was afraid that one of the animals would fall through the roof."

"It was about four miles to the Cedar Breaks where we could obtain water. Our wagon held four wooden water barrels and two or three ten-gallon milk cans. We pumped the water into the cans and Clarence would lift them up and pour them into the barrels in the wagon bed. We got water for the stock from a storage tank. In good weather, I washed the clothes there. (Elsie used a scrub board and homemade lye soap.) On a good day, we had a picnic."

With a forked willow branch in his hands, Theodore walked across the prairie. He had the natural ability to dowse and find water. Gripping tightly, holding it about chest high. Its bark twisted off in his hands. "Clarence, this is where you need to dig your well." Mr. Shaw advised.

It is recorded history that Divining rods appear in the records of ancient Egypt and Rome. Even some Indians used this method.

"The well produced cold sweet water as long as we lived there."

"We planted a few trees around the 'Soddy'; however, what the animals did not eat, the heat and wind was ferocious on the saplings. In the spring, the animals would eat tender greens. Some of the greens were locoweed. When animals ate them, they would stagger, and walk into the barbwire fences. A horse would become loco and impossible to ride."

Homesteaders grew alfalfa, broomcorn, millet, wheat, oats, barley, rye, pumpkins, and potatoes.

"Daddy bragged that they had watermelon on Christmas day as he had buried the melons deep in a haystack to insulate the melons against the cold."

The Rapier and Shaw families were not affected by the flu epidemic in the years between 1918 and 1919. One half million people died of influenza. At least 25 serious race riots had broken out in cities across the nation. President Woodrow Wilson personally led the U. S. delegation to the Paris Peace Talks, which resulted in the Treaty of Versailles.

Everything about the prairie was extreme. The land was flat and treeless, and the sky seemed to go on forever. The tall grass moved in the breeze like ocean waves. Summer brought endless days of heat. Winters were long and cold. Chances of disaster came in the form grasshoppers even jackrabbits, wind and drought, dust storms, floods, prairie fires, tornadoes, hail, cloudbursts, and blizzards. Some events lasted only a few minutes or possibly an hour, then the sun came out, and the cloudless sky was blue. It was a land of contrast with the barbed wire of the ranchers and windmills of the farmers.

Most days on the prairie were uneventful and beautiful with blue skies and bright sun. The young couple fought the eternal struggle of man against Mother Nature.

"I caught a rancher crossing my land," My brother Eugene remembered Daddy telling this story, "after a heated exchange I used a bullwhip on the man."

"Daddy sure could crack a whip, "his son, Eugene commented.

There were still some hard feelings between the ranchers and the homesteaders. Some cowboys thought Daddy was a traitor when he became a farmer. "One night several of them decided to 'hoorah' me and rode up to the 'Soddy' shouting. They did not stay long," Daddy said, "I met them with my rifle."

One morning, I looked out the door," Mama said, "I saw smoke on the horizon. I hurried to the top of the dugout to have a better vantage point to see." In the smoldering heat of summer, smoke on the horizon could mean a prairie fire.

"It was a prairie fire, and it was heading straight for our place. I ran out to the field where Clarence was plowing to warn him. He immediately began to plow a fire lane around our property."

In the smoldering heat of summer, even weeds can ignite a fire by rubbing against one another. There have been fires started from overheated stoves, sparks from a fireplace, broken kerosene lamps, or plain carelessness. To help put out fire cowboys would kill a cow, split it in two, then with two horses drag it over the row of fire. Man, even with his most vigorous efforts to tame the land has not changed these surroundings in a hundred years.

Other dangers to man and animal were Prairie dog holes and snakebites. The burrows the Prairie dogs live in are hazardous if a horse stumbles into one. The horse could break a leg in a hole or his rider thrown. A rattler could strike a cow on its nose as it was grazing. The cow would soon lose its appetite and possibly die.

Prairie dogs, which are a very social animal, live in organized communities called towns. They touch noses to greet or identify each other. The Prairie dogs and rattlesnakes usually live in the same burrow. A rattlesnake can be 3.3 to 8 feet in length, and it is reported that the snake's rattle can be heard up to 50 miles away. The snake can only sense vibrations-they cannot even hear another snake rattle. The snakes eat rodents and other reptiles and can live about 20 years.

"Jackrabbits were another plague. (The critter has enlarged ears and, a hare and is larger than a rabbit.) They were infesting the area and eating the crops. On Sunday, between Kim and Springfield, the neighbors formed a drive to kill as many of the rabbits as possible. The men with horses, wagons, some on foot, others had dogs, drove the rabbits before them.

They either shot or clubbed hundreds of rabbits to death. We skinned, cleaned, and salted down just like pork for winter use."

A common species, the American grasshopper (locust) is about 4 inches long when fully grown. In the fall, females lay their eggs in holes in the ground. The eggs hatch in the spring and the young reach maturity in July or August.

In 1860, Eugene Boe described a grasshopper invasion in "Pioneers to Eternity."

"They came like dive boomers out of the west. They came in the millions with the rustle of their wings roaring overhead. They came in waves, like the rolls of the sea, descending with terrifying speed, breaking now and eclipsed the sun. They dipped and touched the earth, hitting objects and people like hailstones. However, they were not hail. These were live demons. They popped, snapped, and roared. They are dark brown, an inch or longer in length, plump in the middle and tapered at the ends. They had transparent wings, slender legs, and two black eyes that flashed with fierce intelligence."

Elsie pulled a scrap bag out from under the bed. Sitting quite comfortably by the stove, she laid out pieces of material to decide what arrangement of the various colors and patterns looked attractive, carefully arranging all the red tones to one end and all the yellow at the other. She preferred the green and lavender prints. Without the advantage of a sewing machine and electricity, she worked the tiny, meticulous stitching. A sense of accomplishment as well as the artistry, gave her satisfaction as she created a baby quilt.

She cut the material one inch wide, then threaded the long pieces through a shuttle. She braided these together. Later, sewing the braids, Elsie made a small rug to compliment the quilt. The days passed pleasantly for the girl as she was anticipating the arrival of her first child.

"That winter, a storm left several inches of hail on the ground. Ice was a rare treat, so I made Ice Cream," Elsie laughed. "We also melted snow and ice for our drinking water."

When Daddy came back into the warm dugout, biscuits, ham, and gravy were waiting with a pot of hot coffee.

"We were snowbound for several days. Clarence was pacing back and forth. fretting about the animals. However, there was not much room to pace in the dugout." February 13, 1920, a baby girl, Josephine Amanda, was born to the young husband and wife in the little 'Soddy.' They named the baby for the two grandmothers, Josephine Virginia and Rosa Amanda.

One beautiful spring day, Elsie finished milking the cow. She separated the milk, but she still had the cream to churn, however, her youth and good health was making her restless? "I am tired of staying inside when it is so beautiful a day.

Elsie saddled Salem, a sorrel with white eyes, flax mane, and tail, and brought him to the door of the 'Soddy.' She tied the gallon jug with cream in it to the saddle horn. She swung into the saddle with the baby bundled on her lap. Salem broke in an easy trot with his precious cargo on his back. Elsie felt a sense of solitude as she looked out across the vast plain. The Twin Peaks, or Spanish Peaks, loomed in the far distance much as having done since a mighty volcano heaved and thrust them skyward. The Mexican people referred to the peaks as the 'breasts of the world.' It was sixteen miles round trip to the post office. On this occasion, she also made a brief visit to her parents.

"Well, here are my girls." Theodore chuckled and took Josephine in his arms while Elsie climbed off the saddle. Going into the house, he sat down and rocked his precious curly-headed granddaughter, laying his newspaper aside. He had been reading about Warren G. Harding running for president.

"When I finally arrived home that afternoon, Josephine had been lulled to sleep by the smooth rhythm of Salem, and the motion had churned the cream, the oily globules had separated from the gaseous to form sweet, fresh butter."

Daddy would soon be coming in for his supper. Mama busied herself around the stove preparing the evening meal. She made scrapple earlier that morning. All she had to do was cut it in slices, roll it in flour and fry it.

Scrapple
Use five pounds of scrap meat, preferably pork.
In 1 gallon of the cold-water mix in 3 cups of cornmeal
Pepper, Sage. Thyme and salt to taste

Boil the pork in salted water. Remove bones and cut into small pieces. There should be about 3 quarts of broth left. Let it cool than slowly bring it back to a boil as you slowly adding the cornmeal. Cook until thickened. Add meat and spices. Pour into greased pans and cool. Cut slices of the Scrapple about 1 inch thick. Roll slices in flour and fry until crisp on the outside. Serve with honey or syrup or as a side to eggs.

One day, Josephine developed a cough Mama was concerned and sent Daddy to get her mother. "Have you any cod liver oil?" Rosa asked. Elsie nodded. "Give her a teaspoonful every day with a little sugar mixed in it." Josephine soon recovered. Elmer McCollum isolated vitamin D in cod-liver oil and discovered that it combats rickets. The cod-liver oil was the remedy for most ailments of the day.

I remember Mama giving the cod-liver oil to us when we were little. A second baby girl, Theodosia Mae, was born March 11, 1922, a carbon copy of her sister. Theodosia was a namesake for her grandfather, Theodore. However, she was born in the first rock building in Kim, the hotel, which Mr. Shaw had built.

Josephine once wrote of her Grandma Shaw: "*Grandpa built the hotel and Grandma ran it, also did the cooking, I remember she was a good cook and if we had a get together for a holiday or something, she would make the best soup, and bring fresh bread. Grandpa probably kneaded the bread, as Grandma did not have much strength in one arm. It was after my boys were born that I discovered her secret to Grandma's sop. It was Corned Beef.*"

"This country is sure hell on horses and women," Maud, Daddy's stepmother, once noted. "The wind is ruination to a woman's looks and nerves. It dries up her skin until it gets brown and rough like leather. Maud was only in her forties but appear sixty.

"Without the wind though," Jacob said, "there would be no water pumped in the storage tanks by the windmills. No cattle sustained by the water, no life on the flat prairie that holds no rocks, nothing but grass. The sod goes deep into the ground until us farmers plowed up the skin of the earth."

Dorothy Scarborough wrote in 'Cabin Fever':

"It was bleak and bare when the wind blew. Tumbleweeds (Russian thistles) would break loose from the ground and tumble for miles. They stacked up against the fence lines and sometimes broke the fences down. The wind

brought icy blasts in winter and burned them with hot breath in summer, parching their skin, and toughening their hair, and trying to wear down the nerves by attrition and drives them away."

"One of our neighbor women," Mama recalled, "could not stand the relentless wind blowing every day. She went stark raving mad and killed herself. She felt that she was in a prairie prison and cried herself to sleep most nights. The emptiness and wind had frayed her nerves."

"Well, what do you know?" Theodore was amazed at the story he was reading. "James Doolittle completed the first single-day bi-costal flight between Pablo Beach, Florida and San Diego, California. I sure would have liked been there to see that.

"If God wanted us to fly," Rosa retorted, "he would have given us wings like the angels, and you are no angel."

Parties usually held at various homes or the schoolhouse were a neighborhood event to lessen the trials that the people went through. Children slept in a back bedroom or a wagon bed while the adults would dance 'til dawn. Usually, the party lasted until it was time to go home to the morning chores.

Music was provided by whatever instruments were available, usually a guitar or fiddle. At times, Daddy would join in by either cording on a guitar or playing the harmonica, and at times even the accordion.

"But your Daddy loved dancing more," Mama said. "He could dance the waltz so smoothly that he could put a glass of water on his head while dancing and not spill a drop."

"One early morning we were on the way home from a party there was a spectacular display. Electricity in the air caused sparks to come from the horse's hooves and wagon wheels. Streamers of colorful shimmering light were in the northern sky. We stopped the wagon and watched for several minutes. We could see stars behind stars to infinity."

"Another time, I found a woman's beautiful folding fan lying on the road. It was hand painted with birds and flowers. I had no idea who owned such a beautiful item." This fan remained in Josephine's possession for many years.

Josephine wrote, "My brother (Eugene) and I can remember seeing Grandma (Shaw) clapping her hands or slapping her leg in time with music, kept good time too. She had a way of doing a double clap. I used to try to do it but never got it in time. Grandma also would hit two spoons together to make music."

"Grandma told us of dancing at the schoolhouse as a young girl in Oklahoma. Several fellows came in that we did not know. We girls were all scared and afraid not to dance with them when they asked. Finally, the fellows left and had not caused any trouble. We never knew who they were."

"My nephew, George, came to live with us. I had a job hauling freight and did not want to take the kid along. I was well on the road and camped for the night. That darned kid showed up riding on a burro. It was too late and too far to send him back." George deserved the scolding he got.

The homesteaders and the rancher had formed an uneasy truce. Several of the homesteaders in the area were also veterans of the 'World War.' However, some of the settlers who were not well off or had not proved up their claims were moving. The low prices after the War were discouraging to many and their harvest was lost because of a drought.

The Shaw's and Rapier's decided that it was time for them to move too

"Mr. Shaw's car looked like a covered wagon," Daddy recalled. "He had attached bows on the back of his 1922 Maxwell, covering the bows with canvas. Elsie and the babies rode with her parents. George and I each drove a wagon hitched in tandem; with four hear of horses pulling the loads. The trip was going to take us several days to reach Canon City (Colorado)."

The Shaw's settled in Canon City (pronounced Canyon). The Rapier's all moved to the Wall Mountain area west of Canon City. Wall Mountain is one of the many peaks in the Rocky Mountain Range. Their neighbors were Frank Christopher, Dudley Van Buskirk, and Bill Canterbury.

"I must have followed Daddy," Josephine recalled, "for he was down at the corral. I had my head through the pole fence when Grandpa (Rapier) jerked me back. A Billy goat hit the fence right where my head had been. He had butted anyone whenever he had the chance. Daddy kept the goat around to keep fleas away from the stock. Grandpa got the rifle and put an end to that goat."

Clarence and Elsie

9

THE JOURNEY

The Rapiers settled in an area west of Canon City in the mountains where a few years previously a grizzly bear had terrorized the ranchers by tearing down fences, killing thousands of dollars worth of their cattle. A grown steer had no chance whenever the mood struck Ole Mose with a fancy for a taste of beef. Mose killed eight hundred cattle and horses between 1870 and 1904. Three men and possibly eight or nine more died at Mose' actions.

The grizzly, 'Ole Mose', was the king of his day. He headquartered near Black Mountain, Wall Mountain, and Waugh Mountain west of Canon City, Colorado. Mose ranged from Tarryall to Cochetopa Pass about once every thirty days.

Mose had been shot many times and trapped once but suffered only the loss of two toes.

One day Jake Radcliff, an experienced hunter, tried to take down 'Ole Mose'. Mose charged Radcliff mangling Jake's right leg. Mose tossed poor Jake into the air like a cat playing with a mouse. When Jake's friends found him, he was near death's door. They carried him to the Mulock Ranch where Jake soon died of his wounds.

Wharton Pig, who owned the Stirrup Ranch, also tried to kill Ole Mose. Finally, in frustration and desperation, Wharton sent for J. W. Anthony, a professional hunter.

Anthony arrived in Canon City with thirty dogs; he claimed he had used his dogs to kill sixteen bears in Idaho. Were any of the bears Anthony killed grizzlies?

The dogs followed Moses' spoor up between Waugh and the Black Mountains. Then Anthony took several shots at Mose, which did not stop the bear. As Mose came toward him, Anthony figured he was a goner. At that moment, his dogs charged the huge grizzly. Finally, Anthony got a lucky shot in Mose' mouth.

The King 'Ole Mose' died April 30, 1904. Mose was possibly 45 years old, and old-timers in the area said Mose was even older.

Mose weighed between 1200 and 1599 pounds. It took seven strong men to load Mose into a double wagon bed. 'Ole Mose was credited with being the most enormous grizzly ever killed in the Rocky Mountain region, possibly in the United States.

When I was a young child, my parents regaled us with the stories of 'Ole Mose'. I rode my bike to see 'Ole Mose' in the Canon City Museum. I was in awe as I looked up at Mose hanging on a wall.

'Ole Mose' measured ten feet from the tip of his nose to tail; measured across his shoulders and measured nine feet six inches from tip of front claw to tip of front claw. From tip to tip of ears, across the head, was eighteen inches and two inside toes and claws of the left hind foot were missing as the result of Wharton's Pig's steel trap.

Mr. A. Stainsky took the tanned hide of 'Ole Mose' and made it into a rug. The price for tanning, head mounting, and rug backing came to twenty-two dollars and fifty cents.

What a sad and pitiable ending for the majestic creature called 'Ole Mose.' Mose had an honored place in the museum for many years. James W. Anthony eventually willed the trophy skin to the Zoology Department of the University of California in 1987. The catalog number is MVZ #113,385.

"We had a beautiful place on Wall Mountain," recalled Mama. "We could look down the mountain at the clouds below us. I can relate to the stories my mother told about Wall Mountain because I see the same view from my mountain home near Westcliffe, Colorado:

Ghostly shadows of coyotes running through the light of the harvest moon are astounding. At dawn, the coyote's sing while Buck yips and howls, emulates and answers his cousins. Bobcats occasionally poke their heads around the corner of the workshop perhaps hunting rabbits. A dozen feet from the cabin a doe steps into view then slips into the dense forest, which is lush with a thick stand of aspen that mingles with blue spruce, pine and fir trees. The contrasting hues intertwine to conceal the doe.

Blue Jays with a raucous squawk, juncos with twitter, and a squirrel's chitter-chatter greet the day. Beautiful bluebirds flit through the 'quakies.'

The tradition of the natives in the area explains why the Aspen leaves quake. "Christ, on his way to Calvary, passed under the Aspen, and they commenced to tremble and quake in sympathy, and never through the years since then has the Aspen stopped the never-ending shivering."

Early morning sun illuminates the treetops. Intense and dominating the view is a brilliant splash of yellow-gold as a beam of light isolates a few branches of an Aspen. Dew clings to the delicate, translucent leaves as they shiver and quake in a gentle breeze. Precious jewels, the slender stems hold them gently to the branches. A few golden leaves drift hesitantly to mother earth. Some still wearing their summer green frocks are reluctant to surrender to the changing seasons. Only the acridness of wood smoke makes known the intrusion of human existence.

The bark scarred where the elk have rubbed their horns against the trees, and fresh droppings give evidence that the wapiti had made their bed under the pines.

The tiny green body of a hummingbird hovers near with nearly invisible wings. A squirrel darts across the path, a mushroom firmly gripped in its mouth. The squirrel's companion, sitting on a moss-covered rock, chatters away with advice.

At the apex of our 10,000 foot mountain, the panoramic view across the Wet Mountain Valley dwarfs us. A dusting of new snow lies lightly upon the purple Sangre de Cristo range with it numerous 14,000 peaks that sweep as far as the eye can see. Climbing to infinity, they become one with the clouds. Their tops, peaking above the clouds, reach empyrean heights forming majestic mountain islands in the sky.

"It was difficult to grow a garden in the higher altitude. Salt pork, flour, cornmeal, coffee, baking powder, and salt were staples and were stored in buckets with tight lids to keep the mice out of them. We used canned milk when the cow was not fresh. There was abundant wildlife that supplemented the food store. We stored the root vegetables in a root cellar. Clarence loved apples and ate a whole bushel that winter."

"I made cottage cheese," Mama told me. I remember watching while she placed fresh milk on the back of the wood stove to stay warm until it clabbered, and drained it through cheesecloth, add salt and pepper to taste. Sometimes she added cream to the cheese. It was delicious.

"We did not have cash money often", Daddy recalled. "However there were plenty of trees. I would usually hitch 4 to 6 horses with two wagons in tandem. I would chain-lock the rear wheels of the heavy wagons so that they would slide rather than roll; otherwise, the wagon, with its heavy load of logs, could head down the mountain too fast and injure the horses. We hauled the logs to Canon City to sell."

"I must have been three or four," recalled Josephine, "when Daddy took the whole family with him on one trip. There were two wagons, two mules, and two horses all strung out in a line. We had to camp out one night before we got to Canon City. The road wound around the (Priest) canyon. I can remember seeing convicts working on a chain gang. They were building a new route on the side of the mountain. (Canon City is the site for the Colorado State Prison).

I also remember Grandma (Shaw) putting her black fur coat over Theodosia and me to keep us warm when Theodosia squealed with delight and then growled, "I AM A BEAR".

"I was plagued by severe nosebleeds," Daddy recalled. "I thought they were the result of the 'mustard gas' the Germans used during the war. However, a doctor explained that the bleeding was due to the high altitude and dry air."

"I was pregnant again," Mama said, "and we needed to be closer to a doctor. Clarence's nose was bleeding so bad, so we decided to move to Canon City."

Canon City pronounced Canyon) was a name derived from the nearby 'Grand Canyon' of Colorado. Canon City is the third oldest city in Colorado located in a mountain bowl. The Arkansas River flows through this valley, east out from the Rocky Mountains and the mouth of the Royal Gorge on to Kansas.

The Royal Gorge on the Arkansas River, a few miles west of Canon City, is ten miles long and has a depth of more than 1000 feet. The suspension bridge built in 1929 still spans the gorge in spite of the fire that came close to destroying it.

In the meantime, while living at Cotton Wood Box in Canon City Grandpa Shaw received a Tax Notice from Trinidad, Colorado. Vol. P-Z page No. 208 stated that the total due by January 1, 1923, was $30.91 on real estate he owned in Kim, Colorado was valued at $1,480.

The year after President Harding died unexpectedly and Calvin Coolidge assumed the Presidency, Daddy and Mama's third child, Clarence Eugene, was born May 29, 1924."When Eugene was born," Josephine wrote, "Daddy had a hand he had hurt in a sling, and I was sick with pneumonia. Daddy got a woman to come in and help Grandma (Shaw) with the work. Grandma and this woman would work to get things done so they could each go to church. The lady was a Seventh Day Adventist who went to church on Saturday and Grandma went to church on Sunday."

Grandpa Jacob leaned over to light the coal-oil lamp that was sitting on the table careful not to turn the wick up too high to blacken the chimney. The kerosene lantern was brighter than candles. He had bought a gallon of the coal oil from the filling station in Canon City. The filling station had a fifty-gallon barrel of coal oil in a wooden cradle. COAL OIL painted red, decorated the side of the barrel.

Jacob picked up the newspaper his son had brought home and immediately became upset at an article in the paper. "Why can't their husbands keep those blamed women home where they belong?" He threw the newspaper to the floor in discuss.

The article concerned two women, Nellie Ross and 'Miriam Ferguson. They were the first women to serve as state chief executives.

Nellie Taylor Ross was the first governor of Wyoming from January 5, 1925 to January 5, 1927. She was elected to complete the term of her husband William Bradford Ross who died in office. Later President Franklin D. Roosevelt appointed Mrs. Ross to head U. S. Mint, a position she held until 1953.

Miriam Amanda Wallace "Ma" Ferguson served as governor of Texas two non-consecutive terms; 1925-1927 and 1933-1935.

"Can you believe it?" Grandpa Jacob inquired of his son. "They went and elected Nellie Ross governor of Wyoming and "Ma" Ferguson won an election in Texas. That is what you get for giving the women the vote."

"Oh, yes," Maud muttered under her breath, "you would have them barefoot and pregnant."

After the move to Canon City Josephine told this story, "I was four, and Theodosia was two. We decided to go to the store for candy. We knew the grocer would give each of us candy each time we visited the store."

The little girls held hands as they started their adventure. However, as they were about to cross a bridge over the Bessemer Ditch, as they had done previously with their mother they were startled by their mother's voice. "Josephine," Mama's voice startled the girls, "what on earth do you girls think you are doing?"

"Mama gave us girls a stern lecture and we got switched all the way home. We never tried that again." Elsie had been frightened, thinking about what might have happened to the girls if they had fallen into the full-flowing irrigation ditch.

Daddy moved his family to a more substantial house on the other side of Canon City.

"At this house, it was cooler on the balcony, and Theodosia and I would lie on a pallet to nap. Mama made a game of searching the sky to see what animals the clouds looked like until us girls went to sleep."

Daddy had a gentle horse named Salem. "One day, I found Josephine fast asleep on Salem's neck. Salem was laying there sweating. If he had gotten up, he would have stepped on Josephine. I slipped around the stall, reached over the horse manger, grabbed hold of her dress and lifted her gently out of harm's way."

"Well, when Mama found out I got a paddling," Josephine recalled. "Mama always did the paddling. I never went to the barn by myself again." However, this did not deter Josephine's love for the animals.

"One night, a noise woke me up," Josephine recalled. "I thought it must be Santa Claus. I woke up Theodosia. We tiptoed to the door and peeked around it to see what Santa brought us. Grandma Shaw saw us and shooed us back to bed."

The next morning, Christmas morning 1926, they found that Santa Claus had brought a baby sister, Carol June.

> "I see the sleeping babe-hush'd nestling the breast of the mother,
> The sleeping mother and babe-hush'd, I study them long and long."
> Walt Whitman

"Carol was blue and only had a diaper on," Josephine said. "I was petrified and thought the baby must have been very cold." Through the winter, Carol's health did not improve.

"I remember that Christmas a big orange in the top of each sock. It was a treat to have fresh oranges in those days. There were dolls in cradles under the tree, too."

"The baby's heart valve has not closed right. I don't think that she will live very long," the doctor said after examining the baby. "I think that a lower, drier, climate would be beneficial for your baby."

However, Carol was a determined little being and fought to live. She developed asthma later.

Daddy and Mama decided to move to Kansas, where Dad's sister, Jessie, lived.

"We had a little white dog and when Mama gave us a bath our dog thought he had to have a bath too," Josephine recalled. "However, when he got loose he would run outside and immediately roll in the horse manure. Mama would be mad then."

"Daddy made a box on the running board of the car for the dog to ride in during our trip to Kansas but when it came time for us to go, we could not find our dog. We cried great alligator tears until Grandpa Shaw promised that he would find our dog and take care of him". The trip turned out to be a nightmare. Torrential rain slashed at the windshield. Not daring turn around or back up. Dad worried that the car would go off the road into the bar ditch.

"I will use the weeds and tall sunflowers on either side of the road as markers," Dad explained to Mama, "I will drive between them." Finally, Daddy could dimly distinguish lights of a town ahead.

"Say, fellow, where are you folks from?" A man at the Filling Station asked. "You are the first people to cross that flood water in a week." The river had flooded over its banks and put the road under water.

Worry, straining to see in rain and darkness, a sick baby, and three active children under seven took their toll and Mama broke out in hives.

"Sign the register, and I will show you to your room," the woman at the desk informed the family. "Say, what is the matter with your wife?" the woman turned to Elsie, Do you have the measles?"

"You cannot stay here if you have the measles."

The next morning Daddy put Mama and the children on a train. The sun came out. Daddy put the top down on his car. The roads were clear, and he made to Jessie's in good time. Jessie's husband, Lewis, picked up the bedraggled family at the train station and took them home just an hour or so later Daddy arrived.

"My first memories, "Eugene recalled, "were of the family moving from Colorado to Kansas. Aunt Jessie's house set up on a bank and stairs went down to a creek where there was a pretty little pond with fish in it."

Daddy settled his family in Barnes, Kansas, a small town on the Central Branch of the Union Pacific Railroad one hundred miles west of Atchison, Kansas. If you blinked, you might pass the place up without realizing it was there.

"Kansas was unbearably hot and miserable that year. The children came down with a Whooping cough."

"Since your hair is so long and hot on your necks in this heat," Mama said. "I am going cut your hair." Mama cut the girls long beautiful hair very, very, short.

"What happened to your hair?" Daddy was very unhappy. Mama tried to explain that she just wanted to make the girls more comfortable. Nevertheless, when their hair grew long again, he was content.

"The things I remember most," Josephine said, "about living there was going to the store and buying ginger snaps. The clerk would take them out of a big wooden barrel."

"Sometimes we would go to Aunt Jessie's house.

"Mama had whipped up a pudding with a mixture of fresh cow's milk, cream, sugar, vanilla or peaches added for flavoring. Mama poured the cooled pudding into a metal container and nestled it in a wooden bucket. Ice and salt surrounded the container. Daddy and Uncle Louis took turns cranking until the ice cream harden. It was certainly worth it when we tasted the first spoonful of cold ice cream."

"However, one day the ice cream got salt water in it, and due to the cries of frustration, Mama had to make more..."

"Well, what do you know," said Daddy as he read the paper, "Springfield's putting in new streets and there's going to be electricity bringing lights that brightened them after dark."

It was 1927 when the Santa Fe railroad put a branch line in from Satana, Kansas to Springfield, Colorado where Daddy and Mama were married eight years ago.

"Clarence, I have a problem," Lewis told his brother-in-law one day.

"Well, spit it out," Daddy said. "What is the problem?"

"I need help to get rid of rats that have nested under the chicken house." The solution the men came up with was to hook a hose to the exhaust pipe of his car and run it under the building. The children danced around trying to see until the men ran them back to the house.

"Can't say if it killed the rats or not. But it smelled terrible." Josephine quipped.

"One time I went to work for a farmer who had several sons," Daddy recalled. "When we sat down to eat, well, the old man threw the bread to one of his sons, then that one threw it to someone else. No matter where they were sitting the bread was always deftly caught in midair. I never saw anything like it in my life."

After a brief stay at Barnes Daddy had moved his family to Wichita.

Daddy told of a job he had in Wichita at a slaughterhouse.

"We slaughtered the animals first by stunning them with a ball pin hammer then hoisted them to a hook in the ceiling. From that position, the blood drained quickly. We then skinned, disemboweled, and beheaded the animals. We cut the carcasses down the backbone and split it into sides. The sight and smell sickened me. I soon quit that job."

"I went to a little three room school for the first time while we lived there," Josephine said. "In the backyard was an outhouse that had three-holes in the seat, a small hole for little kids, a middle size one, and a bigger one. I was always getting into trouble with the teacher because she said my fingernails were never clean. While living there Mama made something called Lincoln Butter, it was a delicious lemony flavor."

"The house we lived in was close to the Arkansas River. There was just a road between the house and the river. It was the rainy season, and the river was rising. Daddy put a stake a foot or so from the river and every day he would examine the stake to see how high the river was getting. The water rose so fast that we had to move."

"I am not leaving my house," said Mama's aunt, an elderly woman, who lived down the road close to the river. The rising river was creeping closer to her house. When the men went to get her, they found her sitting in her rocking chair on top of a table. She would not leave her home and was more worried about her goats and chickens than she was for herself.

"I will not leave my home!" The men picked her up, chair and all, carried her to safety while she fussed at them.

We moved to Ponca City, Oklahoma. It was a small town in Kay and Osage Counties, named after the Ponca Indian Tribe. It is located in north-central Oklahoma and lies approximately 18 miles south of the Kansas border and is close to the Arkansas River. Ponca City, (New Ponca) was born in 1893 after the Cherokee Outlet opened for settlement in the Cherokee Strip. This event was the most significant land run in United States history. Ponca City is nearby, to other American tribes, including the Kaw, Osage, Ooe-Missouria, Pawnee, and Tonkawa. Kay County, Oklahoma Territory was where Mama's parents, Rosa and Theodore Shaw, were married in 1899.

Grandma and Grandpa Shaw joined us in Oklahoma. Now all eight people were living in a three-room house. The house had an area underneath it that you could enter by way of a trap door under the kitchen sink. This area was convenient for what Daddy had in mind.

It was still the Roaring 20's; Prohibition was the law, a legal ban on the manufacture and sale of intoxicating drinks. Oklahoma was a 'dry' state, and it was illegal to make any intoxicating beverages or sell them.

Nevertheless, to supplement his income and support the family Daddy made homebrew (bathtub gin). "The gin was not hard to make. All I needed was a bathtub large enough to hold water, sugar, rye or corn, something to make it ferment, like yeast."

"Whenever anyone, (especially law officers) came to the house," Eugene said, "someone would tap on the floor, and the light would go out in the basement. Everyone would keep quiet. Grandma Shaw invited the preacher and his wife to dinner on Sunday. The bottles of brew that

Daddy had put under the bed exploded from the heat! What fun! One would pop and then another. Grandma never invited another preacher to Dad's house. Boy, was she mad."

"Daddy's friend, Lee Shore, came to the house one night," Josephine said, "Daddy made him drink lots of strong, black coffee to sober up. The next morning Grandma was taking Theodosia and me to church when she spied a jug standing there on the porch. Lee had left a jug of brew there. Lee Shore was standing on the ground below the porch. Grandma was still angry over the incident with the preacher and his wife. She tried to kick Lee in the head and only just missed her mark."

"She might have killed him if she had hit her target," Daddy laughed.

"Lee Shore's mother was a full-blooded Indian, and she could see the future. She claimed that she knew that a train would kill one of her sons. One day, a train killed a son. After that, she would not tell anyone's future."

"Lee and his wife enjoyed playing cards with Mama and Daddy," Josephine remembered. "They often made Orsta (shellfish) soup when we visited. Sometime in 1929, the folks got a gramophone, which had to be hand cranked to work. Mama made Theodosia and I polka dot dresses, with full skirts. We had great fun twirling them around. If we girls did the Charleston, they would give us nickels. Everyone laughed and clapped while we danced with turned-in knees and toes while we shifted from leg to leg, doing exuberant kicks and wild movements with our arms and hands."

"Lee's sixteen-year-old brother gave us kids fishing pole and took us down to the creek to fish. I saw a big snake in the water. I screamed and dropped my pole and ran back to the house in tears. I was embarrassed when I found out that the 'snake' was just a big frog. Mrs. Shore prepared the frog legs for our meal that day. I was fascinated when I saw the legs jumping in the skillet. Of course, I just had to eat some then."

"On a drive around the country one day," Josephine wrote, "it was just a track between trees and fences, an old horse was in the road, and it wouldn't move. Daddy tried to chase him, but no luck. Daddy said that he would ease up behind him. Well, that old horse kicked the headlight out of our brand new Ajax touring car."

While living in Oklahoma Carol developed asthma and suffered from terrible earaches. We did not know what asthma was at that time. Daddy held Carol and talked to her while smoking his pipe and once in a while he would blow smoke into her ear, which seemed to ease the pain.

. "I had the measles and one day was hallucinating. I saw red snakes going around and around in circles on the ceiling." Josephine remembered. "Daddy brought ice cream home, which soothed me, some. While we kids were all sick in bed, some neighbor boys teased our little dog and made him mean. Daddy was afraid he would bite us and had to give him away."

"Grandpa and Grandma moved to an apartment next door to a Negro school. I thought it was a nicer school than the one I went to."

"A tornado came so quickly one day that we did not have time to go to the storm cellar. Mama put all the children on a bed in the middle of the room while Daddy stood braced against the back door to keep it closed. The garage behind the house had been turned around on its foundation. Also, blown away were the chicken house and outhouse."

Daddy moved his family closer to his work.

"The house was on a dead-end corner of two streets," Eugene explained. "There was one street, then a fence, then a railroad track and another fence. If the drunken Indians going down the railroad track stayed between the two fence lines, they knew that it would lead them home. The Indians in Oklahoma received money for the rights to drill oil on their land. With the exorbitant amount they received, they bought new cars, usually a Cadillac. If they were drunk and crashed their car, they would leave the care where it sat and buy another new one."

"Mama was the disciplinarian," Josephine remembered. "However, there was one exception, when Eugene was four years old, he was found under the davenport smoking one of his daddy's cigarettes." A davenport is a large sofa that stands a little high off the floor.

"Daddy did not buy machine-made cigarettes in those days, so Eugene had to roll this one himself. Daddy rolled a cigarette with red pepper in it and gave it to Eugene to smoke. Daddy was punishing Eugene more for lying than for smoking."

"That day Daddy decided to take us to a carnival at the 101 Ranch. About halfway there Eugene became sick in our brand new Nash. Of course, Mama was still mad at Daddy and mad at Eugene for vomiting in the car. Once we got to the carnival, everything was okay. There were polo games. Daddy sometimes rode in them."

"We saw little horses whose hooves were so small that they could wear silver dollars for shoes," Eugene said. "We also saw Tony, the famous bear. He drank pop from a bottle he held in his paws. It was about 1929-30. A buffalo got a leg broke and had to be hauled away in a sled by a team of horses. Tom Mix was there too with his big white horse. Years later I saw the movies that Tom Mix and his horse Tony were featured. Tom Mix was a famous movie star at that time."

"Then all at once, Mama got scared. She thought that she had left an iron on in the kitchen window," Josephine said, "We got home about the time the fire truck came. The curtains were on fire."

"In those days we did not have air conditioners," Josephine recalled, "so to have someplace cooler than the house we would go down to the river for a picnic.

While working at the Cities Service Oil Refinery, Daddy lost his grip and fell into one of the tanks. "I caught a rope while I was falling and wrapped a leg around it before I hit bottom. Otherwise, I would have been killed if I had hit the hard bottom of the tank."

Daddy developed back problems when we lived in Missouri. He thought it was possibly from the fall he had taken a few years earlier at the City Service Oil Refinery in Ponca City, Oklahoma. He then went to the Veterans Hospital in Arkansas.

"You need back surgery," the doctor told him.

"No Sir," Daddy said, "I will not have you cut on my back. You could paralyze me." No amount of arguing that there was no danger changed his mind. "It's too big a gamble; I am going home." He walked several miles in the rain to return home. He suffered back problems for years but never consented to surgery.

Not long after this accident, Daddy developed a pain in his side. "The fall you had caused this, and you need bed rest," the doctor told him.

"While I was at the hospital, it was winter, and a nurse left a window open which caused me to develop pneumonia," said Daddy.

"Theodosia and I had made a huge snowball," Josephine said. "We had rolled it about two miles home. We got it right in front of the garage and could not move it any further. It was taller than we were." Mama wanted to go to the hospital to see Daddy, but she could not get the car out of the garage. A neighbor man saw Mama's difficulty and came to help, but they could not. He chopped the snowball up and remove it.

"On the road to the hospital, Mama hit a patch of ice. The car spun around and around."

"Whe-eee!" we shouted from the back seat. The spinning was great fun" "Do it again Mama," Eugene requested.

"The car was turned back around facing the direction I came from," Mama said. "The roads had been plowed, but the snow was piled in the middle of the road, so I had to drive back to a crossing to turn around."

"I decided that it was time to go home." Daddy said. "I was sick and tired of being at the hospital with nothing to do. I got up, put on my clothes and walked out of that hospital without the doctor's permission. I kept walking. It was a long way home through the snow, but I finally got home, no worse for the wear."

"I learned to use the sewing machine," Josephine said, "by hemming diapers for the little ones. There was no electricity in the house. The sewing machine sat in the kitchen, and its power came from working a treadle with your feet. Mama was pregnant again and using the machine pedal hurt her feet and back. Mama made our dresses and bloomers from printed flour sacks."

Grandma Shaw stayed up one evening to finish sewing a few items when she heard a noise. Someone was trying to break in. A hand snaked through under the rug that hung over a broken window pane in the kitchen door. It was twisting the doorknob. Grandma screamed then grabbing the scissors off the sewing machine threw them at the door. The scissors struck <u>in</u> the door just below the doorknob. Before Grandpa and Daddy ran into the room the frightened man had run off into the night."

"This was the year that I caught Santa Claus in his long handle red underwear," Josephine laughed. "Grandpa Shaw was dressing up as Santa for us when I surprised him."

"Grandma Shaw was a very stern German woman. Theodosia had done something, and Grandma decided to discipline her. Our house at that time had a walk-in closet that connected two bedrooms. Theodosia in trying to avoid Grandma ran through one closet door and then out to the other bedroom. Grandma was slow, so Eugene and I were able to trap

Grandma in the closet, and then we locked the doors. When Mama and Daddy came home, we were in big trouble."

"I thought the stunt was hilarious," Daddy recalled, "but did not dare show it in front of his wife or my mother-in-law."

"We moved into another house on the same street. Our playground was an old frame of an airplane in the back of the house. We girls slept on a mattress on the floor in one room, and when I (Josephine) tried to stand on my head on the mattress, I hurt my neck."

One evening Lee Shore and his wife came to visit. Mrs. Shore had a new baby. She laid the baby on the bed while they were visiting.

"I had a new doll," Josephine said, "that I just received for Christmas. I wrapped my doll up and laid it on the bed next to Mrs. Shore's baby." When the Shore's were ready to leave, Mrs. Shore picked up the doll 'by mistake,' instead of her baby and started to leave with it. Mrs. Shore pretended to be embarrassed." I thought that I had pulled a good prank."

A stock market crash in 1929 set off The Great Depression. Daddy was fortunate to have a job at all. Nearly one in four people were on a farm. Before it was over, 12.8 million people suffered from unemployment. It seemed that the country had one foot in the field and one foot in a bathtub of gin. In 1930 and 1931, 2,300 banks failed.

We moved yet again to a newer house where Argul Dale was born March 4, 1930, in Ponca City, Oklahoma. At this time, Grandpa and Grandma Shaw were now living in Prichard, Oklahoma so Daddy hired a woman to help Mama with the baby. The custom in this era was that a woman stayed in bed thirty days after a baby was born

"I could not understand why the woman kept telling me that we were out of diapers," Mama commented. "After the woman left I went out to the back porch to do some washing and smelled something very unpleasant. I pulled out a little cot that sat against a wall on the porch. I discovered all the dirty diapers that the woman had not washed."

"To wash the dishes," Josephine recalled, "Theodosia stood on a stool, and I stood on a box to reach the sink. Daddy often entertained us while we washed the dishes. He sat at the kitchen table under the window. He would crow at the little black Bantam rooster to get the rooster in a fighting stance."

The 'Dust Bowl' began in 1931. The rains disappeared, the sod started to blow. Dust clouds reached thousands of feet in the air and Carol became quite ill again with asthma.

"My first memories of Grandpa (Shaw)," Eugene wrote, "was when we lived in Ponca City; He had a Model T Ford one-ton truck. He inserted a hand crank through a hole below the radiator. If this didn't work Grandpa would jack up the left rear wheel then turn it, then the truck would start. It had a gravity fuel tank. If you tried to drive it up a steep hill the gas wouldn't flow to the engine, so Grandpa would turn around and back it up the hills."

"Grandpa and Grandma Shaw either lived with our family or us with them for quite a few years off and on. Grandpa was a jack-of-all-trades. He was a farmer, carpenter, bricklayer, stonemason, and cabinetmaker as well as a rough mechanic. He had to be a mechanic to keep his model T running. He was also an expert plasterer and cement finisher."

"Later Grandpa and Grandma Shaw built a house from railroad ties, mortised like logs, in Canon City. It was just two rooms. Grandpa plastered the inside and stuccoed the outside. Later Grandpa added a frame room."

"Grandpa never used vulgar language. Once he was trimming some trees, his ladder broke. He fell about 15 or 16 feet. The wind was knocked out of him. When he could breathe again, all he said was "Oh Shoot, I did it this time. Eugene I guess you had better take me to the doctor." I was not old enough to driver's license; nevertheless, I knew how to drive."

Many buildings are still standing in Canon City that Grandpa Shaw worked on, for example, the Nazarene Church on the corner of 7th Street and River Street (now Royal Gorge Blvd). That building became a Log Furniture Store.

"One time Grandma Shaw removed a large wart from my foot" Eugene recalled, "by rubbing it with a grain of fresh corn, and then she threw the grain out behind her, so it was lost. The next day my wart was gone."

"When Daddy had a day off he would take us to the river where it was cooler to fish, swim, or have a picnic. A big swing hung from a tree branch that we played on. Grandpa showed us how he could tread water. In deep water, it just looked like he was wading. I decided to go out to where Grandpa was. The water was soon over my head. Grandpa rescued me since Daddy could not swim and did not like to get wet anyway."

"Grandpa and I were very close. He often took me with him, but when we returned Grandma would try to get me to tell her where we had been, I would never tell."

"Mama had some cousins who lived in the country on a big farm," Josephine said. "When we went to visit them Mama would take them some store-bought bread. Their kids thought that bread was as much of a treat as we kids thought that Mama's homemade bread was to us. One day while we were visiting there, Mama had to go somewhere and told me to sew a button on Eugene's pants while she was gone. Their mother showed me how to make a knot in the thread with my thumb and forefingers."

"With the extra money made from his homebrew (bathtub gin), Daddy and Mama planned to visit Grandpa and Grandma Shaw. Daddy and his friend Lee Shore decided to drink up the excess Gin left over before the trip. Daddy gave little taste to Eugene and while we were traveling Eugene sat crouched in the corner of the seat and growled at everybody the rest of the trip."

About this time, Daddy became embroiled in a fight at the Service Oil Refinery with his boss at the refinery and gave the man a severe beating.

The "Dust Bowl' lasted nearly eight years. In 1932, one-fourth of all banks closed and nine million people would lose their savings. Two million Americans lost their jobs.

From the severe dust storms in Oklahoma Carol became very ill with asthma and the folks decided to move back to Colorado

In May 1932, Walter V. Waters and other World War I veterans in Portland, Oregon formed the Bonus Expeditionary Force (BEF) known as the Bonus Army. They demanded payment of money promised to them in 1924 (but not available until 1945.) The veterans were suffering through the Great Depression and needed the bonus immediately.

The Bonus Army left Portland, adding thousands of recruits along the route, and arrived in Washington D. C. at the end of May. About 20,000 veterans gathered at Anacostia Flats and demanded the U. S. Congress provide immediate payment of the bonus. Daddy wanted to join this march, but with his growing family and short funds, it was not possible.

In June, the House of Representatives agreed to immediate payment, but the Senate defeated the legislation. Many veterans left the capital, but more than 4,000 veterans remained in Washington D. C. However, they rioted on July 28. President Hoover ordered federal troops under General Douglas McArthur to end the riot. Cavalry, tanks, and infantry armed with tear gas and bayonets, came into the Bonus Army encampment and destroyed it. The group left Washington after Congress appropriated $100,000 to send them home. Many people scorned General MacArthur for using force to drive the disgruntled veterans away.

In 1936, Congress passed legislation providing for cash payments of the veterans' bonuses. However, Daddy did not receive his until 1945.

"We were moving back to Canon City when Grandpa's truck broke down, so we camped in a field near a creek. At a nearby farmhouse, Mama purchased eggs and milk with the little money that Mama had pinned in her brasserie. We were down to the last of our food. We were a family of nine souls struggling to stay alive."

We arrived in Canon City and camped along the Arkansas River. Mama sold her sewing machine to tide the family over until Daddy found work. We finally moved into a house on South Fifth Street.

The older children were growing up fast by learning to juggle their chores with schoolwork. Mama would get up early to make breakfast, Carol and Theodosia cleaned house, washed the dishes, and helped take care of the younger children. Eugene and Josephine took care of the outside chores.

As a young child, Carol broke her right arm and became ambidextrous. She would do certain things with her right hand and later learned to write, knit, and crochet with her left. She made beautiful, beautiful knitted lace tablecloths.

"We were down to nothing; I mean money," Josephine remembered. "Mama and Daddy took a walk one day. They found fifty cents and that sure meant a lot to them. I remember the first thing Mama bought was salt."

Daddy operated a road grader, fifteen days a month for a dollar a day when he lost his job. Times were hard for the family, and it seemed to be getting harder.

A few days later, Mama gave birth during her eight months to twins. It was a complicated delivery. Gary Arel and Gay Arden were born January 25, 1933. Gary weighed 6 pounds and Gay four. Gary had difficulty and did not start breathing right away.

When the twins were born, Josephine was twelve years old.

"The babies were in a big laundry basket in the middle room,"

Josephine recalled. "The heater was in this room, so it was warmer there than in the bedroom. One day, Grandma Shaw found our big white cat in the basket with the twins. She picked the cat up and threw it the full length of the kitchen and the cat ended up under the kitchen stove. Grandma held the common belief that a cat would smell milk on a baby's breath and that the cat would suck the breath of a baby and cause the baby to die."

Mama stroked the baby's cheek searching for even a tiny trace of color in his pale face. Shallow breathing knifed a whisper of despair in her chest. "Hold on my little boy. Hold on for just one more day." Gary only lived 18 days dying from a cerebral hemorrhage. February 12, 1933.

Morning Song
Love set you going like a fat gold watch.
The midwife slapped your foot soles,
and your bald cry took its place in the elements.
I'm no more your mother than the cloud that distills a mirror to reflect
its own slow effacement at the wind's hand.
All night your moth-breath
flickers among the flat pink roses. I wake to listen:
a flat sea moves in my ear
Excerpts from a poem by Sylvia Plath

"Why did God take this baby?" Mama struggled to understand. "The other children are healthy, except for Carol's asthma. Even Gay is healthy although so tiny."

The Canon City Daily Record reported:

"One of Rapier Twins Taken By Death Tuesday. Gary Arel Rapier, three-week-old son, of Mr. and Mrs. Clarence T. Rapier of 839 Fifth Street died at 5:45 Tuesday morning. The baby was one of the twins, a boy, and a girl, born to Mrs. Rapier on January 25, 1933. The baby girl is getting along nicely it is reported."
The body of little three-week-old was laid to rest in Lakeside Cemetery Wednesday afternoon following services at the Wilson Chapel. The Rev. J. W. Wells pastor of the Nazarene Church

A MEMOIR OF THE RAPIER'S

conducted the services at the Wilson Chapel. (Rapier, Gerry (sic) A. Infant, sec. 14B-BLK002-Lot 001-GRV001 2-15-1933.)

"That year on Memorial Day," Josephine wrote, "we wanted to go to the cemetery. Mama had a dime she saved for a long time but used it to buy gas for the truck so that we could go. We lived quite a distance from home to the cemetery."

Gay Arden, Daddy's little China Doll

Tunnel Drive is above the Arkansas River. A railroad track is on the north side of the river where Daddy found a granite stone that had apparently fallen from a train car. The stone weighed between 50-60 pounds. Grandpa Shaw carved the inscription Baby Rapier in 1933.

Daddy placed it on the grave of his baby son.

Jacob Asbury Raper may have been part of the majority that celebrated in South Canon, Colorado when the 21st Amendment ended national alcohol prohibition on December 5, 1933.

In Oklahoma, Kansas, or Texas the combination of wind, heat, and lightning or static electricity from the dust and combustible grass was nature's perfect recipe for a fire in those areas. The tumbleweeds blew against fence lines and dwellings. In the old world, the thistle or tumbleweeds, was 'perekati-pole.; which meant 'roll across-the-field. The seeds of the thistle had clung to the clothes of the German/Russian immigrants. The immigrants came from the old country, to America with the seeds embedded in their clothing. The seeds were transplanted to our soil when the immigrants became homesteaders.

"Thank God we did not live in those troubled states." Carol was healthier now in Colorado.

Franklin Roosevelt's primary vehicle to be elected, in 1933, as President was "The New Deal'. The 'New Deal' was a package of social and political programs that restored economic health through the nation. The CCC or the Civilian Conservation Corps was to give jobs to a small army of young men to build road, bridges, culverts, trails, cabins, and entrance stations and sewage lines. Some of these works can be seen to this day at the Mountain View Cemetery in Pueblo, Colorado. The rock wall, surrounding the cemetery, was constructed by the CCC during this period.

"Does anyone want to see a jackass?" Daddy would ask. He then would pull a dime from his pocket with Roosevelt's likeness engraved on it. He disliked Roosevelt intensely and blamed Roosevelt for many of the veteran's problems. He thought Roosevelt was a dandy with the tilted cigarette holder and a funny accent.

The Social Security Act established a federal pension for retirees in 1935.

Daddy often saw 'Baby Doe' Tabor dressed in bib-overalls driving a truck on the streets of Canon City. Baby Doe was not recognizable as the raging beauty of former years who was married to Horace Tabor worth $9,000,000. Famous in the annals of Colorado is the rags to riches story of Horace and Baby Doe. Baby Doe survived the sinking of the Titanic. Her husband long dead and penniless, Baby Doe was found frozen to death in a tool shed at the Matchless Mine in Leadville, Colorado in March 1935.

"When Grandpa Rapier and Daddy got together, they often sat up all night talking about old times and people they knew. They had fantastic memories and could recall what a person looked like and what they said. All night sessions story telling became a family trait. Daddy would fish out a sack of Bull Durham from his shirt pocket and roll a cigarette. There was a big, red and white snorting bull on the packet. We always tried our best to stay awake and listen to the stories told."

"My Dad and I were sitting on a bench in front of his livery stable talking," Daddy related, "when we heard a tobacco-spitting fellow, with a black beard, make a comment about a young girl who was walking up the street toward us. Before I could get up to take the man to task, Dad pushed me back and backhanded the man and knocked him to the ground.

Grandpa Jacob stood over the man, "and you will show more respect for a woman in the future."

"The man had made a comment about Jessie Mae, my sister". The man did not know he had been floored by a former Deputy US. Marshall. There were stories told about Grandpa's adventures as a Deputy Marshall in his younger days.

Jacob always thought his uncle Marquis B. Rapier was someone to look up to and emulate. Marquis (Mark) served with the Republic of Texas from 1827 through 1829. So sometime in his early life, Jacob became a United States Marshall.

An area in Oklahoma territory was one of the last places in the United States where an outlaw could hide, and never be seen again. In the late nineteenth century this corner of the Panhandle, 'NO MAN'S LAND' served as a roost for outlaws thieves and killers.

"Well, Jacob, I need you to go after a horse thief down in the Oklahoma Territory. The punishment for a "loose" woman was usually banishment from the community. A man's first offense was a lashing applied fifty times with a hickory switch or a rope. If it was a second offense 100 lashes were administered. However, a third offense, depending on the severity of the crime, could be anywhere from tar and feathers, lynching, or being shot down like a "dirty dog."

Jacob brought back the horse but not the man. It was the man's third horse stealing episode, and Jacob saved the expense of a court hearing and hanging.

On one occasion, Jacob was sent to arrest a Negro.

Standing in front of the man Jacob said nothing; his weathered face was enough to scare the man who started fighting. Instead of shooting the fellow, Jacob picked up a half-brick from the ground and hit the man upside his head.

"I did not mean to kill him. I only meant to stun him enough to subdue him. Nevertheless, the man died."

Grandpa Rapier and Maud moved up on Copper Gulch in Custer County, a rugged county a few miles southwest of Canon City.

"We were on our way up Copper Gulch to visit Grandpa Rapier," Josephine said, "when the car broke down. Daddy left to get the truck and had to hitchhike back to Canon. Mama made something for us to eat. She built a fire under a flat rock, and when it got hot, she cooked hamburgers on the stone. She always took food up when we went to see them."

"Another time, coming home on Eight Mile pass, the lights went out on the car. It was dark and raining. Daddy rode on the fender and held a flashlight so Mama could see to drive. Eugene and I used to like it when we went in the truck. We would use our peashooters to hit the road signs. We got pretty good at it too."

"Another time when we were there (Grandpa Rapier's) Eugene and I got on a horse to go for a ride. Coming down a slope Eugene got his foot in the horses flank. We bucked all the way to the barn. Daddy and Grandpa saw us coming, ran out, and caught the horse before he ran into the barn. It would have knocked us off, as it was a low door. We would have got hurt. That poor horse had its tongue hanging out."

Grandpa Rapier lived near Hillside in Custer Couty just a few miles South of Canon City when at age 80, died on November 25, 1935, On his death certificate it states that he lived near Westcliffe, Colorado which is a few miles South of Hillside. He is buried at Lakeside cemetery in Canon City.

At home, times were hard, but we had planted a large garden, which helped supplement our income. The carrots we raised were washed, cleaned, and sold for five cent a bunch, which was about one pound each. The older children picked blackberries, strawberries, and gooseberries. Mama stayed very busy canning this produce. Before she had a pressure cooker, she used a hot water bath to do her canning. One time, after the twins were born, a family with a sick baby summoned Mama to help. Mama sat up nights and nursed their baby along with Gay. When Mama was leaving, not even a 'thank you' was offered.

"I was about twelve years old," told Eugene, "when Dad had a Dodge truck. The front and body were an Essex. It was a mixed-up vehicle. One evening Dad and Mama talked about going to Tucson, Arizona." (Probably to get a load of something.)

"Our car was out of gas, so Dad decided to drain some gas from the truck. The truck's gas tank was under the seat. Dad got a piece of canvas, and a bucket crawled under the truck and lay down on the canvas. Taking the drain plug from the gas tank, he accidentally dropped it. Daddy asked me to strike a light so he could find the plug. He had put his thumb over the drain, but some of the gas dripped on his sleeve."

"Well, I struck a match! Dad came out from under the truck spilling the bucket of gas, which burst into flames. His clothes were on fire! The canvas was on fire! Dad rolled quickly on the ground to put the fire on his clothes out. Dad had first and second-degree burns. I still have the pocketknife that Dad had in his pants pocket that night. The knife had Celluloid handles, and one side was burned off."

Celluloid, originally the trade name and is now a standard name of synthetic plastic. In the United States, celluloid was invented by John Hyatt, who was trying to win a $10,000 award by finding a substitute for ivory in making billiard balls. He did not win the prize.

Celluloid is transparent and colorless, and in the paste, the form can be colored, rolled, or molded into specific shapes. Some of its advantages are that it is inexpensive and durable, takes a high polish, does not warp or discolor, and is not affected by moisture. It is, however, FLAMMABLE, and although modifications in manufacture have reduced the dangers of fire, other materials have mainly superseded it. Celluloid is used in the making of combs, brushes, and buttons.

Blood had left a stain on the floor. Grandma Shaw could not remove the stain no matter what she used. From that time on, she kept a rug over that spot so no one would see the stain. One day Eugene was playing in the yard when he found a handgun. We children always believed that someone was murdered, in our house, with the gun Eugene found.

Mama suffered a miscarriage about this time. When she was in the hospital, Eugene developed a lump on his leg.

The doctor explained that it was housemaid's knee and applied some paste on it. (Coal tar?) It will draw the fluid out. Eugene was up running and jumping in no time.

Of course, Eugene was embarrassed when we teased him about his 'housemaid's' knee.

January 30, 1936, on Graydeen Ave. in Canon City, the eighth child, Alton Elwood, came into the world without any difficulties.

The family worked hard to make ends meet. Women who had large families had to buy and prepare fresh food daily, Mama and Grandma canned produce from the large garden behind the house. They had no labor-saving devices such as electric washing machines, refrigerators, dishwashers or vacuums, crock pots, or blenders. There was no television to entertain the children.

"Clarence worked in the coal mines for a time and always came home full of coal dust," Mama recalled, "I had the galvanized tub full of hot water ready for his bath and helped to scrub him down."

Coal mining was hazardous and physically draining. With undercutting rock, boring holes for charges, laying tracks, lumbering installed in rooms, or loading thousands of pounds of coal into cars, Mama was frightened that Daddy could have a crippling accident. Some men were permanently hunched and had chronic back problems. There was also a chance of death and injury from explosions or fires caused by dust or methane gas. A man could be crushed or buried by rock falls. Mama had many nightmares and begged Daddy to quit working in the mines.

"Between 1913 to1933 the fatality for every thousand miners in Colorado were 5.02 compared to the national average of 2.96. -- - Few men could spend a substantial amount of time in a mine without being seriously injured—many were scared for life." (Coal People by Rice J. Clyne)

Daddy could not find work after he quit working in the mine. He had relatives in Missouri who told him he could also make a good living cutting wood. He made the trip to Missouri to inquire about chopping timber and farming. He thought that at least on a farm the family would have food to eat.

He returned to Canon City, and we moved lock, stock, and barrel, to Missouri. On the trip, Daddy took the truck taking Eugene and Argul with him. Mama drove the car that pulled a trailer. Josephine took care of the little ones for her mother. The family arrived in Missouri to find disappointment; the land that they were to have and cut wood on was now unavailable.

A MEMOIR OF THE RAPIER'S

We located on another farm where the house had an unfinished porch on the front of the house. Not long after settling in the place a tornado came. Daddy saw the storm coming, grabbed a canvas, and told us all to run to the timber. The furious funnel carried the roof away. We ran back to the house. Before the rains descended on us, Daddy placed the canvas over the dining room table, and we all huddled under it. It was the only place dry in the house.

After the storm, I stepped on a rusty nail when Mama sent me to bring the children in," Josephine said. "Mama sat up all night putting a hot linseed oil poultice on the wound to pull out the infection."

Daddy bought a few cows from a man. "Oh, those cows are fine. They don't need to be tested." He swore. "They are healthy."

Daddy always said a man's word was his bond, so he believed the man. Daddy had to destroy several of the sick cows, to prevent a disease from spreading to the other animals, losing money and cows on the deal. Daddy became quite ill with Undulant Fever. Daddy always swore that is what caused him to lose his hair.

Undulant Fever, also known as Bangs disease and brucellosis, infectious is a disease caused by various species of bacteria of the genus Brucella, transmitted to humans from lower animals, especially cattle, hogs, and goats. Human beings acquire the disease through contact with infected animals or by drinking raw milk. Weakness, with chills, and high night fevers often results in central nervous system disorders, painful joint, and miscarriage, characterize the acute form of the disease.

Grandma Shaw and Mama had many remedies for various illnesses.

This handwritten Recipe for Neuritis (or rheumatic fever) is in an old cookbook of Mama's featuring a "Home Comfort" Range Model DA.

3 oz. Powdered Senna   2 oz. Powdered charcoal   1 oz. slippery elm bark
*   9 powdered)*
3 oz. olive oil   1 oz. glycerin   3 lbs figs (half-white, half black)
*   1 1/4 lbs raisins*

Cut stems from figs and raisins, mix in the powders, add glycerine and olive oil and mix thoroughly with liquids, form into balls the size of a nickel and put into a glass jar. Take one ball night and morning on an empty stomach for a week then take one ball a day for six months (1 course).

Daddy acquired an excellent riding horse that he named Tony. One day Daddy decided that Tony could pull the cultivator, a completely foreign concept to Tony. Tony reared up, then fell back on the cultivator cutting one of his legs. Sometime in Daddy's life, he had worked for a veterinarian and had a talent for the healing of animals. He soon had Tony healed and never used him in such a manner again.

"I remember one time, I was helping Daddy to doctor a sick cow," Eugene said. "She had gotten into some grain and was bloated. Dad put a hose down her throat and poured some liquid down her, and then he put a hose up the other end and flushed her out. Tony, our horse, developed a sore on his neck. Dad gathered herbs to make a paste to apply to the sore, the sore healed but left a hole, but his mane covered it, so it didn't show." Bert, a grandson, inherited Daddy's veterinarian tools.

"Mama, Theodosia and I were standing at the back door," Josephine recalled, "watching storm clouds fathering when lightning struck a wire fence nearby, and it ran along the fence until a post obstructed it, then it ran to the ground. The charge threw us down to the floor."

"Well," Mama commented, "I guess we won't be doing that again."

"Mama, Theodosia, Eugene and I," Josephine remembered, "were baptized in a creek. It was a regular old-fashioned kind of baptism with singing and shouting."

The barn had a scene of mountains painted on the door. To obtain household water we walked across a fallen log over a creek, and there were several apple trees on this place," Josephine said. "Daddy sold apples for fifty cents a bushel. A man who came to spray the trees traded work for apples. We had a neighbor who had chickens, and he wouldn't keep them penned up. The chickens would get into our garden and scratch everything up. One day Daddy invited the neighbor to dinner, we had chicken and dumplings. We ate lots of chickens that year."

"As we were new to the neighborhood, Daddy wanted Theodosia, Carol and I to meet others our age. Daddy took us to Tin Town where a dance was taking place in a schoolhouse. The people there were very unfriendly and acted as though they were suspicious of us. The boys sat on the wall and stared at us."

"Daddy danced with each of us, but we were not enjoying ourselves. We never went back again. Theodosia and I attended Strafford school for a time."

A MEMOIR OF THE RAPIER'S

That fall there was rain, rain, and more rain. It rained every day for thirty days. It was so muddy that to get to the main road to town with the car, Daddy then had to hitch a team to it and pulled it out to the main road. On the return home, he would maybe get the car halfway up the long driveway and then hitch the team up again to pull it the rest of the way home. Josephine and Eugene helped Daddy with the outside work while Theodosia and Carol helped Mama with the household cleaning and caring for the younger children.

One day, Daddy drove the team while cutting corn. He had built a sled with a long scythe on one side to pull behind. When a bundle was ready, Eugene would hand it to Josephine who tied it. A leaf from the dry shocks of corn hit Daddy in his eye. For a time, he was afraid he would lose sight in that eye.

Grandpa and Grandma Shaw traveled from Colorado to visit. Mrs. Hathaway, a friend of theirs, came with them as she had relatives near Springfield that she wanted to see. Grandpa had a Studebaker touring car. He rigged it the same way he had done with his 1922 Maxwell when they left Kim. We kids laughed because the car looked like an old covered wagon. "We stopped overnight on the way," Grandpa chuckled as he told the story, "the next day I noticed something flapping behind the car. That old lady (Mrs. Hathaway) had washed her long underwear and hung them on the back to dry."

Move! Move again! It was a farm with more acreage and a larger house, which was a blessing for the growing family. That winter their ninth child arrived. I, Elsie Arlene, was born January 26,

1939. Daddy and Mama's journey contains many chapters, but this is where this chapter ends.

The next place the family lived in had a barn that someone had painted a scene of mountains on the door. To obtain water for the household by walking across a fallen log over a creek. Josephine and Theodosia attended Strafford school for a time. Mama, Theodosia, Eugene and I," Josephine remembered, "were baptized in a creek. It was a regular old-fashioned kind of baptism with singing and shouting."

One day Mama was pregnant with her ninth child when she snapped.

Tearing her clothes off she ran to the barn where she threatened to kill herself with a pitchfork.

"Josephine," Daddy shouted. '"Quick, bring a blanket to cover your mother."

Daddy picked up Mama and carried her back to the house. Daddy sent Mama sent to Grandpa and Granma in Colorado for a much-needed rest. Grandma had volunteered to take care of the two youngest children, Gay and Alton, while Mama regained her health.

"It was after my Mother died that I was told this story by my brother, Eugene and also by Josephine,'" said Arlene. "I wonder how much it would have effected me in my younger years. I know that mental health was not discussed in those days. Mama had several episodes of nature through the years."

Mama finally sent word that she would arrive home on the train in Springfield, Missouri on a certain day. The letter arrived the same day she was due home," Josephine recalled, "I saddled Tony and rode to tell Daddy. He was working on another farm where we would be moving to in the fall. While I was riding Tony, (sic) decided to race a car with some boys in it. Tony was so strong that I could not hold him back."

"When I finally got Tony stopped, I walked him quite awhile cool him off and calm down myself. Boy, did I catch it from Daddy when he found out!" Tony came to me when I shook a bucket of corn or oats in it or when Eugene would whistle."

Everyone was glad to see Mam home again and looking well.

"Within a year after I was born, the family moved back to Colorado where we lived with Grandpa and Grandma Shaw for a short time north of Canon City," said Arlene.

The Journey Continues

My Parents were true nomads or else had a drop of gypsy blood. I often wondered why we moved so often. The places I mention in this work are but a few.

A MEMOIR OF THE RAPIER'S

Excerpts from a poem by Thom Gunn:

ON THE MOVE
One lacks direct instinct before one makes
Afloat on the movement that divides and breaks
One joins the movement in a valueless world,
Choosing it, 'till, both hustler and the hustled,
One moves as well, always toward, toward.

I tried to count all the places that we lived after I was born; it was between fifteen and twenty. I attended eleven different schools. It seemed that I was either ahead or behind the new school curriculum. I never made close friends and still have a hard time doing that as an adult.

One day, Daddy was working in the barn when he smelled smoke and glanced toward the house and shouted, "Elsie, get the kids and get out of the house. The roof is on fire." Sparks from the fireplace caused the fire to ignite the roof.

Daddy leaned a ladder against the house then climbed to the roof. Mama pumped water at the well. The older girls carried the buckets to Eugene on the ladder. Eugene then transferred the water to Daddy. Finally, the fire was out however it left a six-foot hole in the roof. Daddy patched the roof and walled up the fireplace then installed a large wood stove.

"Of course," Josephine told, "that ruined the baby's (Arlene) playing with the charcoal. She would pick up the charcoal from the fireplace and eat it."

"We (Josephine and Theodosia) graduated from the Fair Grove School. Nevertheless, we didn't get to do the cap and gown bit. Just a few days before graduation, the folks decided to move once again."

Carol's asthma was terrible, and Argul had developed hay fever, so Mama and Daddy planned to go to Oregon and homestead on land that was still available. The plan was fruitless as they only made it as far as Canon City where Grandpa and Grandma Shaw lived.

Daddy made a bargain to look after the clubhouse at Shadow Hills Golf Club just a few miles south of Canon City on Oak Creek road. At the time it was empty and for rent. The course was very primitive. The 'greens' were sand! We certainly did not know anything about golf." Years later, Josephine married John Delly who was a semi-go-pro and managed golf courses.

Josephine and Eugene would take the twenty-two rifle, their dog, and go hunting quite often. Both were excellent shots. While tramping the hills their dog would run down a rabbit. "Daddy got word that a mountain lion had been recently killed nearby, and after that forbade us to go hunting alone again."

This is some of Mama's home remedies:

Suck on a piece of clove to alleviate a toothache
Drink Sassafras tea to thin blood on a hot day.
Plaster of Turpentine and kerosene or mustard plaster
apply to the chest for a cough or cold.
Soak hand in kerosene to toughen and protect hands.
(Grandpa Shaw used this every day.)
Drink a hot toddy for a <u>Chest</u> cold or the flu.
(A hot toddy is a drop of whiskey in hot lemon and honey water.)
Note: Mama did not allow whiskey except for medicinal purposes.

I was about two years old when Mama noticed that my skin was red, spotty, bumpy, and scaly. Blisters developed, which burned, and itched terribly. The doctor diagnosed Scarlet Fever. The doctor lanced a couple of blisters, which resulted in scars on my neck and the back of one knee.

The rest of the children, except Eugene, came down with the fever. Eugene was working at Bolt's in town. When he returned home, Mama could not let him in the house. We were in quarantine that lasted two months. In the meantime, Eugene stayed with Grandpa Shaw.

"We moved and scrubbed the house from top to bottom with Lysol," Josephine remembered. "Even the piano did not escape the treatment."

The next move was to a place on Four Mile Road east of Canon City. There were several milk cows. The family bottled the milk and sold it. Daddy invented a bottlebrush attached to a motor, which made the chore of washing the milk bottles easier.

Looking into the man's eyes, Daddy reached around for a rag to wipe his hand. "Okay, Pop with have an agreement. I will raise the hogs on shares." Barehanded with calloused palms, Clarence shook hands with "Pop" Ireland (sic).

This was customary to look into each other's eyes and with the press of the flesh. To make kept. However, one day, when we were gone, the man took all the hogs and sold them. Daddy did not see any profit from the sale or his hard work.

Daddies never used swear words around Mama or us girls.

"But he let loose with a few choice words in the barn," Eugene recalled.

This photo best represents my father.

However, Theodosia did not want to wear her skirt over her shorts. When Daddy saw her, he was mortified. He said he would not walk with her and not for her to expect him to defend her honor. I remember Theodosia put the skirt on."

For a short time we lived near the Bessemer irrigation ditch in Canon City, Alton started the first grade at Roosevelt Grade School.

In 1931, the specter of war once again hung over the world, in 1935, the Nazi government passed the Nuremberg Laws, which deprived all Jews of their citizenship and forbade them from marrying Gentiles. The United States was neutral at the time. United States citizens were warned to travel at their own risk in the war zones. By 1940, Germany invaded Denmark, Norway, Holland, Belgium, Luxembourg, and France. Germany then marched against Russia.

Daddy and Mama read about an impending war and were worried about their sons. It had only been twenty-one years since World War I when on December 7, 1941, Japan launched the attack on Pearl Harbor. December 8th Congress declared war on Japan. December 11th Germany and Italy declared war on the United States.

Mama and Daddy received a letter and photograph, dated March 6, 1944. It was from Mrs. Eleanor Roosevelt, President Roosevelt's wife.

Canon City Daily Record Wed, April 12, 1944
Mrs. FDR sends photo of Sailor to family here to Mr. and Mrs. C. T. Rapier, 1215 South Fourth Street, Saturday came a prized souvenir from the White House, Washington. A personal letter from Mrs. Eleanor Roosevelt and with it a large photograph taken in Brazil of a picnic at which their son, Bugler First Class C. E. Rapier sat at the head table with Mrs. Roosevelt.

Mailed in a White House envelope and personal signed by the President's wife, the letter read:

"Dear Mrs. Rapier;

On my recent trip to the Caribbean and South Atlantic Areas, I had the pleasure of meeting your son. I thought you would be glad to have word of him and to know he looked well.

I enjoyed so much the luncheon we had at your son's station, and Captain Roper has suggested that you and the other mothers of these boys might like to have a copy of the photograph taken at the time.

The signed photograph which I am enclosing goes to you with my best wishes for your boy, sincerely yours, Eleanor Roosevelt."

A MEMOIR OF THE RAPIER'S

Roosevelt, seated, at a table with eight sailors in which Eugene was one of the eight. Seventeen-year-old Eugene joined the Navy in 1942.

Above the photograph, apparently written in Mrs. Roosevelt's handwriting is the inscription 'Picnic Luncheon, Atlanta's Grove Tejipis, Brazil, March 16, 1944.

The picture shows the long picnic table at which sit Mrs. Roosevelt and Naval Captain Walter Gordon Roper, flanked on either side by eight sailors, one of whom is C. E. Rapier of Canon City. All autographed the photo. Rapier is seated two spaces away from Mrs. Roosevelt.

He attended local schools, entered the Navy in Dec. 1942. He was with a vessel of the Pacific Fleet and has been on foreign duty for the past nine months. He is now stationed with the Naval Unit at Tejipis, Brazil. He will be 20 years of age may 29.

"Why change things?" Mama remembered a quote from Anne Ellis, "a sow's ear is valuable to the sow, while a silk purse at best is an ornament." In other words, "You can't make a silk purse out of a sow's ear."

"Women were just starting to wear shorts in public," Josephine recalled. "Theodosia and I made an outfit with a skirt to wear over the shorts. Wearing our new outfits, we decided to go.

Josephine and Theodosia left home to work at Peterson Field near Colorado Springs. Josephine worked in an office and Theodosia worked on the planes. Josephine met John Delly, a New Yorker, who was in the Army. Theodosia went to Utah where she was a telegrapher for the railroad as a telegrapher.

I was probably was three or four when we lived on 17th street in a house west of ours lived a boy named Artie that was my age. Artie's father was painting their house when Artie and I devised a game. We put our handprints all over, as high as we could reach, in the fresh paint. I do not know what Artie's punishment was, but Mama certainly lit into me.

One day a man came to the house to talk to Daddy about our dog, Rex. He was looking for dogs for the army. We were upset and cried. Of course, Daddy did not allow the man to take Rex. I had learned to walk by holding on to Rex by the cuff Mama had cut off Daddy's trousers and slipped over Rex's neck.

Carol and Gay had the bed, and I slept on top of a trunk. One night I tried my hardest to stay awake waiting for Santa Claus. Nevertheless, I fell asleep. I do not remember what I received for Christmas. I just remember the magic of that night when I was positive that I had heard sleigh bells. Alton finished the first grade that year.

Seventeen-year-old Carol ran away from home. I do not know if it was because Josephine, Theodosia, and Eugene were gone and she wanted to prove that she was also a grownup. Mama and Daddy later learned that Carol had joined the WAC's and was in Walla Walla, Washington driving trucks. Carol joined the WAC's, a member of the Women's Army Corps, a division of the United States Army that existed between 1942 and 1978. While there Carol fell in love with one of the German prisons at Walla Walla, Washington. Of course, nothing came of that love.

I learned that no matter who came to our house or whose house we went to, I sat still and did not speak unless someone spoke to me. If there was a bowl of candy sitting in front of me, I knew better than to touch it or take a piece without permission.

Mama was a great one for making notations or putting poems in her Bible. This was one:

Psalms 9:13 "Have mercy on me, O Lord; consider my trouble which I suffer of them that hate me, thou liftest me up from the gate of death."

I do not know who Mama imagined hated her.

A MEMOIR OF THE RAPIER'S

In the photo below are:

Chief Johnston, C. T. Rapier, Geo. Hokiness, Walter McKagan, John ---ssalage, Perry Johnson, Alva Allen, Joe Willson, Gill McNarilly, Geo. Bird, Raymond Orff, Jack Limons, Earl Goodween.

(I apologize if these names are incorrectly spelled.)

Daddy worked at Pueblo Ordinance Depot east of Pueblo. He was a mounted guard and later was in charge of the remount stables. Josephine came to visit.

"I went out to see Daddy at the Depot who as a mounted guard patrolled the area. I was surprised to find our old horse Tony there." Tony remembered the girl who once rode him like a wild Indian. "Daddy got me a pair of his pants to war, and I was able to ride Tony one more time."

There was a write-up when Daddy had straddled the door of a Jeep and roped a little antelope. He quickly made a pet of it and had a nanny goat as its surrogate mother.

ARLENE JANOSKI

Daddy learned other skills, his blue-cross-stitched tablecloth was a treasure for many years.

Tony offering advice.

Eventually, the horses were retired, and the guards became motorized. We soon moved back to Canon City on Fourth Street. My brother, Argul, loved to tease Alton and I. His favorite taunt was calling us 'Two Gun Pete with stinking feet.' Nevertheless, he would protect us. We had a Shetland pony tied to the clothesline behind the house when some dogs tried to attack it. Argul and Rex fought the dogs off.

Daddy's stepmother lived just across Bessemer Ditch from us. We kids never called Maud our Grandma. The large ditch provided water to farmers downstream. Maud's grandson Dicky lived with her, and I thought he was the meanest kid alive. He was about Argul's age. One day after shelling some pea's mama threw the shells into a hole in the backyard. I was sitting there playing with the pea shells when Dicky threw a big rock at me hitting my knee. Argul straightened Dicky out fast.

One day, Mama asked Argul to give Alton a ride to school on his bike. Alton was in the second grade. Either Argul forgot, or he did not want to be pestered by his kid brother. Mama took the razor strop with her and went to the school and found Argul. Every time Argul rose up to pump on the pedals Mama smacked him on the bottom. He never forgot again. Mama firmly believed in the philosophy SPARE THE ROD. SPOIL THE CHILD.

"Argul was not the only one to get the razor strop," Josephine recalled. "Eugene got it once when we lived on Greydene. Mama had sent me to get the boys, but they didn't listen and didn't come in. Mama gave Argul a spanking and then took after Eugene with the strap, whipped him all the way under the bed. I was plenty scared; I thought she was going to kill him. Through the years I also received a dose of that strap."

Bessemer ditch was very dangerous. It had no fence to prevent children from falling into it. A young child fell into the ditch. The searchers could not find the boy. Argul took Rex, and they swam in the ditch and finally located the child's body.

"Mama baked a cake, which was a rare occurrence, sugar was rationed during the war." I still have the old Ration Books they used. Mama frosted the cake then sat it on the kitchen table. She was gone only a few minutes, however, when she returned the cake had disappeared. Mama accused us kids of eating the cake. Rex cowered in the background behind us. Mama then noticed that his muzzle still had frosting on it. We thought Rex was just one of us and tried to shelter him from Mama's wrath."

Mama and Daddy did not know quite what to think when Josephine introduced her boyfriend. He was as alien as he were from the planet Mars. He was easterner from New York and of Italian descent. One time Johnny bragged about all the beautiful women in New York. Daddy quipped, "Well, why did you have to come to Colorado to find a wife."

On October 23, 1943, Josephine and John were married at our house in Canon City.

"Johnny brought presents for everyone. My present was a beautiful doll and gave Alton a B-28 bomber airplane. I was jealous because I wanted a plane too. There was a curtain hanging in the double doorway from one room into the living room. I used my doll to put on a play to get Johnny's attention. I thought he was very handsome."

We all went over to visit Maud While there I had to use the outdoor facilities, and Maud lent me a flashlight to go to the outhouse. While admiring her sheepskin seat cover over the hole; I guess Maud's bottom got cold sitting on the wooden seat; I dropped the light down the hole. Maud became extremely upset that I had lost it. She wanted Johnny to retrieve it. He politely refused, and we went home.

"I remember what I thought was a giant. The giant was just a boy who came to visit. He was so tall that he could rest his arm on the edge of the porch roof."

"Mama had to put blackout curtains on the windows. The Air Raid Warden would come by to check if any lights were showing from the windows at night. I was frightened when the air raid siren would go off during the night."

"Mama received news that Grandpa Shaw was in an accident. Grandpa and Grandma were riding with Pete (Grandma's nephew) and his wife, Nora. A sack of walnuts tied to the back of the car caught fire from the exhaust pipe. Grandpa was getting out of the car to investigate when

Pete let the clutch slip. The door opened toward the front. T The car suddenly lurched forward, (March 8, 1944) the door caught Grandpa and knocked him to the ground.

Grandpa Shaw was born in Indiana on February 25, 1870, spent his earlier years in Kansas before coming to Colorado. He was married on May 20, 1899, to Grandma, Rosa Fansler, who is living.

Grandpa died in his h on Monday, April 10, 1944, of Bronchial Pneumonia. In failing health since falling from a car. He was 74-years-ol.

A MEMOIR OF THE RAPIER'S

And died at his home at 1418 Greenwood Avenue, at 9:10 o'clock Monday morning. Grandpa Shaw is buried at Lakeside Cemetery in Canon City

He had resided in Canon City for the past 22 years, coming here from Las Animas County where he homesteaded there in 1915. During his residence here, Grandpa Shaw worked as a cement contractor and was a skilled workman along that line

A few years later Grandma Shaw married Elisha J. Sullivan. The Sullivans had been longtime friends. We grandchildren never called Grandma by that name, It was always Grandma Shaw. and we never called Mr. Sullivan grandpa.

Daddy's job transferred him to Utah. He went ahead leaving Mama to pack and follow later. However, when Daddy arrived at the new position, he discovered that he would have a women boss. He quit on the spot. Daddy found employment at an ambulance company in Ogden, Utah. At this time, Carol was also working in Ogden.

Argul built a big wooden box in the backyard to pack things in. Argul had quite a time loading the box on to the trailer. But with Alton's help, they managed. Mama was going to drive the car and pull a trailer. Even with this, four children and Rex, she was not a bit intimidated and headed off to Utah.

Mama could be very resourceful.

There was a time when the sediment blub, on the car developed a crack. (Sediment from the fuel settled in the bottom of a glass blub.)

There was no help forthcoming on the lonely road. Mama's ingenious method of repairing the bulb was that she had we children chew bubblegum then used the gum to patch it until we limped into town to have it replaced.

If my memory as a four-year-old is correct, on the road to Ogden in the middle of nowhere Mama drove under a railroad bridge I saw wonderment or dreamed it. I observed a group of lions, laying in the shade of that bridge. I asked Alton if he remembered the incident, but he does not, and told me I must have been dreaming.

In the years since I have driven over Highway 50 between Colorado and Utah many times. Always after entering the moonscape of the desert, I have marveled at the wonder of it and always looked for my lions.

We moved into Washington Terrace just on the outskirts of Ogden.

The houses which all looked alike, were barracks-style with living quarters on each end of the building, which was confusing to me. One evening, after a long day of playing and exploring, I walked boldly in on a family that was not mine. That night, I met Marie who was my age. When school started, we were in the first grade and had many adventures together. Her mother walked me home to the other end of the building. Alton was in the third grade.

To my way of thinking, Gay was the perfect child who never got into to trouble, unlike me. For example, I noticed that my first-grade teacher's hair was slightly askew, so I laughed. I had never heard of a wig much less seen one. The teacher marched me to the front of the class and smacked me several times on my open hand with a ruler. I would not cry so she shut me in a dark coat closet until I 'learned my manners'. However, I explored that closet and soon discovered a balm to my misery, a bag of candy, which I promptly consumed. Of course, that meant a note to Mama. I did cry when Mama made use of the old razor strop.

Gay had a beautiful China doll, and without her permission, I took it outside to play. Of course, when it became dirty, I decided to give the baby a bath. I left it to dry and forgot it. When Gay discovered it, the poor thing had tiny cracks all over the face. It was ruined! She was furious. I do not think she ever forgave me this offense.

Carol married Norman Robinson, a Navy man, August 29, 1944. Tommy was born August 29, 1945. I fell in love with the tiny baby with dark, curly hair and brown eyes. I thought I was a perfect little mother. I would give him his bottle and help change his diapers. To this day I still tease him about that.

Daddy worked at the ambulance company where he drove the ambulance and taxi. We do not hear much about polio now, but in that year, polio was running rampant. Polio, infantile paralysis, is a contagious disease caused by a virus that attacks the central nervous system, injuring or destroying nerve cells that control muscles.

Daddy had transported several children, contorted with pain, to the hospital with polio and he was terrified that his children would also contract polio, but our family was blessed as none of us contracted the dreaded disease.

One day, Alton and I took a bus to see Daddy at work. Why? I cannot remember. Alton must have been eight and I five when we got off at the corner. As we were crossing the street, an ambulance came tearing around the corner. Daddy was not driving. Alton pulled me back just in time, or I would have been hit. You must remember, we were not city kids only country 'bumpkins' But, I always wondered why Mama let us go to town in the first place.

Daddy did not have but a third-grade education, but he devised an ingenious way of counting the coins at the end of his shift. He put each of his fingers onto a penny or a dime, then quick as a wink he had the money added up. Seventy-three years later, I still have some of the coin wrappers that Daddy used.

My memory also told me that Gay was about eleven when she became deathly sick. I remember how scared I was when I could hear her throwing up and seeing a wash pan full of bloody water Mama carried out of the bedroom. When I tried to ask Mama what was wrong with Gay, she just hushed me and sent me away. I heard the whispering about a woman's problem. I never did find out what was wrong. Gay did recover but always seemed to be delicate after that.

During the summer months, I followed Alton everywhere like a puppy. Gay and I were never very close. She was close to Argul though. When we were not annoying them, we found other things to pique our interest. We played and explored most days until we were exhausted by night. We caught grasshoppers and putting them in empty fruit jars.

One day, while I was making mud pies, I looked up to see a sailor swaggering down the sidewalk. I ran into the house shouting, "Eugene's home! Eugene's home!"

Josephine and Johnny came to visit then. Daddy and all the fellows were in the living room, and

Daddy was showing Johnny his rifle. Not knowing that Daddy always kept his guns loaded, accidentally, Johnny fired it. He was sorely embarrassed. He was a veteran and had seen fighting in the Pacific.

This incident only upset Mama even more at her son-in-law. Johnny had earlier teased her by asking when she was going to fill the empty pie shells sitting on the counter. We knew to watch what we said to Mama, as we never knew what would upset her.

We did not have kindergarten then so I was in the first grade, and winter was nose-nipping. I was walking home one day when I discovered a beautiful cocker spaniel frozen to death. I ran home crying for Argul or Alton to help the puppy.

Daddy played the Harmonica occasionally. His favorite tunes were 'Strawberry Roan,' 'Coming through the Rye,' and of course 'Rye Whiskey.' He could imitate a 'Jews Harp' by producing two notes at the same time. One a deep drone and the other was a whistle-like, high-pitched, overtone melody.

Josephine recalled, "The songs I remember Daddy singing or humming were these."

> *In the twilight glow, I see her*
> *Blue eyes crying in the rain*
> *As we kissed goodbye and parted*
> *I knew we'd never meet again.*

Another that Dad sang was Hank Williams's song: "I'm So Lonesome I Could Cry."

> *Hear that lonesone whipporwill*
> *He sounds too blue to fly*
> *That means he's lost the will to live*
> *I'm so lonesome I could cry.*
> *And as I wonder where you are*
> *I'm so lonesome I could cry*
> *I'm so lonesome I could cry*
> *I'm so lonesome I could cry.*

"Even today every time we hear these songs I think of Daddy."

Daddy could not really whistle. I never could either although I really tried. He used to, what I call a whisper-whistle which he would do when occupied with his work. Daddy showed me how to whistle using an empty twenty-two shell, the same principle as blowing into an empty pop bottle or jug.

Vocal music is the primary source of musical expression of the Siberian people. Among the Turkic-speaking Tuvans in southern Siberia, a form of 'throat-singing' is practiced and believed to be an imitation of the 'Jew's Harp.' I do not know where Daddy learned this art. Daddy also made music by placing a thin piece of paper over his comb and blow on it.

Daddy often chuckled when he recalled the story about Grandma Shaw at a dance when she was a young girl.

"I was dancing," Grandma Shaw once said, "having a good time. In that day and time, it was fashionable to wear a long dress that was tight around the ankles. Every time I passed a certain man, sitting close to the dance floor, he tried to stick the toe of his boot under my skirt. Well, I had enough and slapped the man."

"Mr. Shaw said she actually cold-cocked him."

After Eugene was discharged from the Navy, he purchased some farmland near Cortez, Colorado. Therefore, we were on the move once again.

Just before we left Utah, I was playing with Marie. I was probably teasing her and locked myself in our car and would not let her in. She threw a rock, which made a small hole in the back window. We kids told the story about that the hole was from someone shooting at us.

It was a dry-land farm, which means that there was no irrigation system. You relied only on the rain. Daddy, Eugene, and Argul worked hard trying to raise wheat and corn. It was so hot and dry that summer the corn and wheat did not even peek out of the ground.

Alton took water bags to the field where they were working and I as usual tagged along.

There was no electricity or plumbing in the house. The boys carried well water was in the house. Mama did the washing in the galvanized washtub that we also took our Saturday baths in. Each child bathed in order of our age. Of course, I was the youngest and sometimes dirtier than even Alton. Mama washed Gay's and my hair with Castile's Hard Water Soap then rinsed it with cider vinegar, which made our hair soft and shiny. Our long hair created problems at times. When playing under the scrub oak brush a tick embedded in the back of my neck. Mama got rid of the Tick by tipping a small jar of ammonia or turpentine over it until it backed out. Mama examined us regularly for the little monsters. Mama would have cut my hair, but Daddy would not allow it.

One night, I had an urgent need to go to the outhouse. I do not recall why I just did not use the 'Thunder Mug that was under the bed. If you have never heard of a 'thunder mug' go to a museum and you will get an education on the use of such. The 'thunder mug' had to be emptied and cleaned every morning, which chore sometimes fell to me.

Mama told Gay to take me to the outhouse. The night was very dark. There was no moon showing at all. I stepped on something that was wigging across the path and jumped. We saw a rattlesnake slithering into the dry grass.

Oranges were wrapped in orange-colored tissue paper, and we were thrilled when Daddy brought home a box. We had either an old Sears and Roebuck catalog or that tissue paper to use in the outhouse instead of the modern toilet paper we have today.

Everyone had a chore to do. I usually cleaned the lamp glass chimney of the lamps, which I did not mind. However I got more black on me than on the cleaning rags. I finally learned to clean them with newspaper when we had it. I detested cleaning the 'thunder mug.'

I am terrified of snakes; this is the result of that hot summer on the dry-land farm. Alton teased me with water snakes found in the irrigation ditch on Aunt Ruby's farm near Durango. We had to look carefully for snakes before we stepped off the porch. Rex attacked a snake before it could strike Argul. The snake bit Rex on the tongue. His head was the size of a basketball. Daddy put Rex in a root cellar, swabbed his mouth with a kerosene rag, and fed him eggs and milk until he recovered. Rex lived six more years. I think Daddy once said that we killed twenty-one snakes that summer. To this day, I cannot stand to see a snake on television or look at a photo of one.

That hot summer Mama had a bushel of apricots, with the weather being so warm she did not want to use the kitchen; she decided she could dry them instead. Her method of drying the fruit was to stretch bed sheets over a set of sawhorses. She halved and pitted the apricots then layered them on the sheet covering them with another to keep the flies and bugs from the fruit. In just a couple of days the apricots was dried and ready to store.

Mama's Dried Apricot Pie:

> ¾-cup sugar
> Two cups dried apricots
> 1 ½ cups of water
> 1-tablespoon butter
> Soak the dried fruit in water for several hours, or overnight, and cook slowly without sugar until tender. Dredge prepared lower crust with flour, put in a layer of fruit, sprinkle generously with sugar, alternate the fruit and sugar until crust is filled; distribute butter over the top layer; adjust the top crust and join around the rim with moistened edges; dredge top lightly with flour and bake in moderate oven until well browned. Latticed strips of pastry may be substituted for the top crust.

Argul somehow had an old car, possibly a Model T or something like that, that he would drive around the farm. He would pretend that he was John Dillinger, the infamous bank robber. Gay, Alton and I were his gang. Dillinger gained nationwide notoriety during his short career, from June 1933 to July 1934, as the country's most wanted criminal.

With the failure of the dry-land farm, Mama and Daddy were ready to move again. Josephine wrote to them that there was work in Connecticut where she lived after Johnny was discharged from the army. Josephine was also expecting twins, and Mama wanted to be there to help.

Mama canned everything she could for the move, even chicken. We still had the seven-passenger Buick so with Mama, Daddy, Eugene, Argul, Gay, Alton and I not forgetting Rex, there were eight bodies in the car. Pulling a trailer, we were off.

"The trip from Cortez, Colorado to Norwich, Connecticut was quite an undertaking," Eugene wrote. "We ran into a blizzard going down the river road from Salida to Canon City. We stopped for four days at Grandma Shaw's, then on east to Connecticut where Josephine lived. Dad and I went to work for a small construction company. Dad and I worked that winter next spring back to Canon City."

"In Wheeling, West Virginia we stopped at a motel. It was rainy, and Daddy was not wanting to get wet ran from the car to the office of the motel. The motel manager locked the door, pulled the shade and would not answer."

Daddy and the boys always wore western wear; boots and hats. Daddy had not shaved for a couple of days. I suppose the man thought that Dad was one of those wild-west characters.

I remember that Mama carried the money pinned inside her brasserie. She was sure that it was safer there than in Daddy's pocket.

We then traveled through New York City the tall building and overhead railroad dwarfed us. The traffic was horrible. Rex jumped from side to side, over us kids, looking at the sights. Our eyes were round at the wonder of it all. We had never seen buildings more than two or three stories high. I thought the trains would crash down on us.

Alton was in the 4th grade, and I was in the second. We enthralled the other children and teachers with our stories of the Wild West that we had lived in. We showed them the hole in the back window of the car telling them that outlaws had shot at us. We told stories of stagecoaches, bank robberies, and so forth. We said that we were Indians and would scalp them if they crossed us. Who believed our stories? Anyway, we had no problems.

Josephine lived on the Thames River near Hartford, Connecticut. There was an old Indian fort (Fort Uncas?) a mile up the dirt road to her house that we explored hoping to find relics. Across the river was an 'insane asylum' and Johnny would swim across that wide river and back quite often. I am surprised that he never was run over by the ships and submarines traveling to the Navy Base upriver.

Josephine had a cat that had fleas. Alton decided that the only way to get rid of the insects was to throw the cat as far as he could into a cove along the river.

That Christmas I crept out of bed and sat on the top steps to listen to everyone talking. I anticipated the wonderous things Santa would bring. I guess someone must have put me back to bed. My present was a new nightgown that Mama had made.

In the vast attic in their house, Johnny had built a set of train tracks for the new arrivals. Josephine had twin boys, John Daniel and Joseph Francis, March 27, 1947.

I do not know what the occasion was, but Jonny parents came from New York for dinner. Josephine made spaghetti and meatballs. Eugene would not eat the spaghetti as he said it looked like worms. I am sure it must have hurt Josephine's feelings, but we had never eaten spaghetti before.

I remember Mama was upset because Johnny's father wiped his mouth on the edge of the white tablecloth.

One night, we rode on a ferry boat to New York to visit Mr. and Mrs. Delly. Mrs. Delly had a five-course meal. Alton drank a big glass of what he thought was water. However, it was anise, liquor. Mr. Delly entertained us after dinner by playing a small accordion (Concertina?) Mrs. Delly told me there was something on the bed for me. I walked back into the dark hallway and scared myself by seeing my reflection in a full-length mirror. There was a baby doll on the bed there first real doll I can remember having all my own.

There was another time Daddy set his foot down on Mama. At school, the teacher forbade the chewing of gum; nevertheless, I was anyway and tried to blow the biggest bubble. When the bubble popped, it went all over my face and in my long hair. Mama wanted to cut my hair short, but with Daddy's proclamation, she had to work hard to get all the gum out.

We arrived in Connecticut in September 1946 and left in the spring of 1947.

In 1948 we were back in Canon City, we lived in a four-room house on Ussie Street. The main floor of our house was four rooms. The door between the kitchen and a bedroom locked. The boys slept in an unfinished basement. Argul found us a bicycle somewhere that was a joy to ride. We had a neighbor (Mrs. Fiecoat (?) that complained of the noise we kids made. When one of our balls bounced into her yard, she would not give it back until Argul went over to talk to her. What the conversation was about, I have no idea. That was also the year I was introduced to 'spin-the-bottle.' Of course, my friend was always the one the boys chose to give them a kiss.

That year there was a Prison break from the State Prison on the west end of Canon City. Daddy worked at the prison for a short time but did not relish the idea of escorting a prisoner to the gas chamber. One night, while he was patrolling the yard the Warden Roy Best's Doberman Pinchers were loose and tried to attack him. Daddy had a gas pellet gun, which he shoved down the throat of one of the dogs killing it. It was a mutual agreement that Daddy left that job.

"That night," Alton recalled, "I was riding my bike around Canon City and did not know about the break until I came home. The radio announcer warned people to stay in, lock their doors, and not venture outside."

A day or two after the convicts were caught Gay and I was in the kitchen doing the dishes. Mama, Daddy, and Argul were gone at the time. Alton was in the bedroom. Evidentially he decided to pick up the rifle when it went off. A bullet went through the door and hit the dishpan in Gay's hands. We never told Mama and Daddy about the incident. It was one time I kept shut. Mama probably wondered how the hole got in the dishpan.

Of course, Daddy always kept his guns loaded. We knew better than to fool with the gun. HA! HA!

After the convicts escaped, we learned that they entered the house of a friend of Grandma Shaw's. The convicts tied up her husband and instructed the woman to cook them a meal. The woman found, an opportunity to hit one of the men over his head.

When we lived on Ussie Grandma, and Mr. Sullivan's house was on Myrtle in a house that backed the place we lived on. One day we heard Grandma screaming and running through the gardens to our house. She and Mr. Sullivan got into an argument about their pension money. Grandma had hit Mr. Sullivan on the head with a poker. She did not kill him, although I think she tried.

I think after this we lived in a tiny town in the mountains called Hartzel for a short while. Alton went to school in Fairplay, and I went to school across the street in a white schoolhouse. I remember that Alton and I rode bikes all over the countryside and caught suckers in the small stream meandering through town. One day Alton and Rex came home smelling to high heaven of skunk. Alton and a friend were riding horses while chasing a skunk. He said the skunk swerved, the horse served, he did not. Mama gave Alton and Rex a bath in the washtub in the yard then applied tomato juice to try and kill the smell. I think they had to sleep outside for a few days.

Also, when it got cold Daddy nailed a dynamite box in the window to keep the milk cold.

I also remember the grand occasion of seeing a solar eclipse for the first time. The teacher warned us not to look directly at the sun. We mad visors from cardboard with narrow slits cut it the board to look through at the sun.

We lived on the Ford Mountaindale Ranch the year there was a Presidential Election. Daddy did not like the Democratic Party. Mama never told Daddy that she had voted for Harry Truman. Later, Daddy came to respect Mr. Truman for his "the Buck Stops Here" philosophy.

Argul was working in Canon City, and Gay stayed with him to finish school. Argul was probably about eighteen and Gay about fifteen. Gay still has bitter feelings about this time.

Alton was in the sixth grade, and I was in the fourth at the Star Lytle School. As far as I know, this was the last 'one room' schoolhouse in the state. We always bragged that there were nineteen children, counting the teacher because she was about nineteen years old. I wish I could remember her name. She was very young and beautiful, and I hoped that Eugene would marry her. Our school bus was an older car that a man drove to all the ranches. Alton said there were six kids he picked up. Two lived on the Turkey Creek Ranch, one lived Stone City. One boy's name was Neil Addington (?).

Our teacher always encouraged us to finish our work quickly and then we would go outside. She would play ball or some other game with us. We were in a Christmas play that year, however, on the way home, Alton and I were in the back seat of the car when he pulled out a toy snake that rattled and scared me to death. I almost killed him before Daddy could screech to a stop.

On this ranch, we had cows, goats, pigs, and horses, my favorite horse an old gray called Gus. Daddy knotted a rope to tie to the saddle horn that I could climb up on to the saddle. Gus would let go up on the mountain to bring the cows in but when he was tired there no stopping him from heading home. Gus was afraid of crossing a bridge, sheep, and blowing paper. It was several miles to the mailbox, and the boys usually rode Gus or another horse there.

Daddy and the boys hunted, and Mama canned what they brought home, usually a deer.

My least favorite animal was the old Billy Goat. When Billy saw me in a skirt, he would try to butt me. One time he ran me up on a hay wagon to get away, and I tore a skirt that Mama had just made me. I complained to Alton. Alton and I devised a plan; we took biscuits and crumbled them to entice Billy to a pen. Alton took his small baseball bat climbed up on the railing and hit Billy on his head. The bat bounced off Billy's horns. He might have had a headache, but that was all the ill effect he sustained. He was undaunted and still tried to butt me when he had an opportunity.

We moved back to Canon City in the house that Grandma Shaw had lived in at one time <u>on</u> Myrtle. Sometime before this, Mr. Sullivan died. Gay and Argul were with us again. Argul had a friend named Bob Singleton. Gay and Bob eloped one night. They were married May 25, 1949. Gay had turned sixteen the 25th of January.

We moved up to Prospect Heights that was a little further up sour and west of Ninth Street. This where Eugene would lie down to read and eat an apple and Rex would lie down beside him and eat an apple. We lost our old faithful dog that summer. When Rex was dying, Daddy put him under the galvanized washtub and gave him Ether.

That summer I tried to show off to a neighbor girl on the bike. I was wearing shorts at the time, and I was skinned, up head to toe. My bed was a cot in Mama and Daddy's bedroom, and I guess Alton thought I was knowledgeable about certain things. He asked me if his penis was as big as Daddy's was. I did not know what he meant.

We had a mare and her foal that we called Tiny. When we moved again, we had to leave Tiny behind.

The Korean War loomed.

Eugene decided to enlist in the Army. He tried the Navy again, but he did not qualify as he had a few back teeth pulled over the years. Argul wanted to enlist, however, due to his hay fever he was considered ineligible. Daddy hada job at Hill Air Force Base south of Ogden, Utah, so we moved again. We lived with Carol and her second husband, Harold Ekstrom, for a while. Carol and Harold later moved, and we stayed at their house that year. Daddy and Mama had some friends they liked to play cards with. When they played Canasta (?) Alton, and I played with them. That is until I caught Alton hiding a card under his bottom on the chair. 'Sarge' just laughed but his wife got upset. Mama would not play with them again. But 'Sarge' was a neat guy and liked us, kids. He even lent his new

Chrysler to Daddy when we had to make a trip back to Canon City to see Grandma Shaw.

Alton attended North Davis Jr. High in Layton and I was in the sixth grade at the Syracuse Grade school when I was Betsy Ross in a school play. I was nervous, had practiced, and practiced my lines while doing the dishes. Mama had curled my hair around her finger making long curls. I hated finger curls. That was the last time she curled my hair. My photo was in the paper, but Mama never saved it. Alton and I both had the Mumps. Alton was sicker than I was and stayed bed for a while.

That cold winter at the bus stop there was a boy who I thought weir. His hair was wet from his morning shower and had frozen every day that winter.

Mama was fifty years old when she started smoking, and Mama and Carol tried to hide the cigarettes packages by wrapping them in a handkerchief and burying them deep in their purses. They did not realize the smell lingered.

Carol was married to a Mormon man. Mormons do not believe in smoking. Of course, neither one seemed to realize that the smell clung to their clothes. Mama became a chain smoker. There were times I followed Mama around from one room to another putting out her cigarettes. She developed emphysema, bronchitis and eventually kidney failure. From this experience I never smoked.

Daddy never said anything to Mama, or if he did, I never heard it. Daddy smoked, however, it was one cigarette after breakfast and one after dinner. Occasionally, he smoked a pipe or a cigar, but Mam would not allow the cigar smoking in the house. He also took a chew when he was working with his animals. I used the empty Prince Albert cans to hold many little treasures or crayons.

Earlier when we lived in Canon City that Prince Albert can come in very handily. I was coming home from school a neighbor girl, who was Alton's age, was a bully who decided it would be fun to pick on me. She tried to hit my legs by swinging her metal man-sized lunch pail. I was carrying a paper lunch sack, which contained a Prince Albert can, a glass bottle of glue, and other items. I hit her over the head with my sack then ran as fast as I could home I knew Alton would protect me. She then developed a crush on Alton, when he did not reciprocate; she put a turd in a sack on our front doorstep. That girl was a bane to my existence as long as we lived next door to her.

Daddy took Mama to Dr. Tanner for her nerves. Mama tried to tell us that the doctor had prescribed for her to smoke for nerves. Dr. Tanner was a Melchizedek Priesthood holder in the Mormon Church. He would not have said such. That. Daddy confided to me that Dr. Tanner had advised him to hospitalize Mama. Daddy felt that it would be a disgrace to do so. Now, as the only girl left at home, Daddy asked me to keep an eye on Mama when he was working.

When I started menstruating, I thought I had hurt myself playing football with the boys. Mama would not talk to me. She sent for Theodosia to come home to explain what I was experiencing. However, the terms Theodosia used I did not understand. However, soon after there was a Disney film shown at school that clarified all the details about becoming a woman. Mama was horrified when she found out

We were expecting company. Argul was bringing a girlfriend home, to meet the family, for the first time. Mama made her special sauerkraut dinner which made our mouths water. We all sat around the table talking and enjoying the meal. Florence was a small woman, blue eyes blondish hair, and quiet. She ate a small amount of the dinner. Argul married Florence Johnson January 21, 1951, in Elko, Nevada. Florence and I became good friends, and she took me to church, the Church of Jesus Christ of Latter Day Saints, with her. Years later Florence and I laughed when she confided that she did not like sauerkraut.

It was a cloudy day when Argul was swimming. He laid on the shore to rest and fell asleep. When woke up he had a severe sunburn. He called Mama to see what her remedy would be for the burn as he developed large blisters. Mama treated him with cold tea compresses. He could not wear anything but shorts for several days.

The Korean 'Police Action' was escalating, and Argul received a draft notice. They did not care that he had hay fever now.

As we saw Argul off on the train. he said, "Daddy, this will probably be the last time we see each other," Argul whispered.

Argul was in a camp back east for a short time Josephine invited

Florence to stay with her in Connecticut so she could be closer to Argul before he shipped out to Korea. Florence was now pregnant.

By the next summer, we moved to a part log and Cinderblock house near Clearfield. I visited Theodosia and her husband Frank at their home in Jackson, Wyoming. Theodosia was a beautician and Frank, and his father had a clothing store. While I was there, I had the mumps again. Theodosia cut my hair, and I never grew it long again. While I was sick, I stayed in the back room of the clothing store and Frank treated me to ice cream from the shop next door every day. One day, Theodosia asked me to go to the grocery store for her. I held the twenty-dollar bill in my hand the wind blew the money out of my hand into a gully. I could not find it and was in tears when I went back to the store. Frank noticed something was wrong. When I confided what had happened, he gave me money to go back to the store and cautioned me not to tell Theodosia.

When it was time to go home, Frank gave me a new coat and took me to the train. It was the first time I ever rode on a train. I was so thrilled that I could not sleep. Alton was to meet me at the station in Ogden. However, he walked right by me. At first, he did not recognize me as I was dressed differently and had short hair. We went home by the 'Bamberger,' an electric train,'

The next year in the seventh grade, I became acquainted with a Japanese girl in my class who played the violin beautifully. I admired her and desperately wanted to play the violin or cello. When I went into the music class, I discovered that the other students had been playing their instruments for several years. I was embarrassed and did not go back. If that experience tainted my talent for music, I do not know, but I cannot even carry a tune when trying to sing hymns in church.

I also had a teacher who intimidated me. She was a big 'German' woman. She punished the students by making them bend over between the desks, letting the other students hit them on the bottom with a yardstick. One morning, it came to my turn; I refused to submit to the punishment. I thought it would be humiliating as it was the custom then for girls to wear dresses.

After a visit from my father to the teacher, she did not use that form of punishment again.

One of the biggest thrills was going to the drive-in=movie. Stanley

Adams, Alton's friend, drove his father's automobile although he was not old enough to have a license. Stanley could barely see over the steering wheel. We would all pile into that car and Stanley would drive us to take to the drive-in. He knew someone there who let us in free. The song played before the movie started was 'Hold That Tiger' by Les Paul and Mary Ford.

While working at the Hill Air Force Base, Daddy was showing a fellow how to do his work correctly. He was standing between a tractor-trailer and a bulldozer when the man on the bulldozer let his clutch slip. The bulldozer jumped forward pinning Daddy between the equipment breaking his back. It was a miracle that Daddy had not been killed. The small thing that might have saved Daddy was his wallet. It was in his back pocket as he was crushed against the tail light of the semi.

The doctor applied a full body cast on Daddy by laying his head on one table and his legs on another which caused a sway back. This was so miserable that when Daddy came home, he made Mama and Alton cut the cast off with his pocketknife. He never went back to that doctor. Ther after, he suffered back problems for the rest of his life. He would lie on the floor and have someone pull on his legs to relieve the pain. At this time, he also developed double vision.

After Daddy recuperated somewhat from the accident, he was on his way to work, when a sudden vision came to him.

"Argul's face was right there, and it startled me," Daddy said. "I almost wrecked the car. I turned the car around and came home. I know something has happened to Argul."

One night soon after this incident, a telegram came. Argul died in the conflict in Korea on September 2, 1952, the day Daddy had the vision. Daddy went into the backyard. That was the first and only time I ever saw my father cry.

We were later told that a lieutenant stepped on a landmine, Argul was following close behind. They were both killed instantly.

We left and moved from Utah and returned to Canon City. I do not know. We lived in a two-story white house on Elm Street just a couple of blocks from 'Dead Man's Corner.'

The family all returned to Utah to be with Florence when Argul was buried November 4, 1952 in Ogden, Utah. It was a closed casket, and

A MEMOIR OF THE RAPIER'S

Mama could not believe Argul was dead. She was afraid the Koreans had captured him. She thought he would come home someday.

When we returned home, Mama was having difficulties. At this time I was in the eighth grade and stayed at school for a tea party Mrs. Finger, my teacher, was giving for the girls in my class. After it was over Mrs. Finger offered to drive me home. When we entered the door, Mama sitting at the sewing machine was so startled that she started to throw the scissors at Mrs. Finger. I called out just in time to stop her.

Mama really became disturbed when Eugene announced that he was going to marry Florence, Argul's widow. Eugene had never met Florence until Argul's funeral. Well, Mama always thought that Eugene would stay a batchlor and take care of her in her old age.

One day it was cold with snow on the ground when sMama climbed out of the bathroom window. We did know where she was for several hours. Daddy found her at a neighbor's house.

packing plant in canon. One night Alton and I went to town just driving around in his coupe. We saw some girls walking up the road. They were going home after seeing a movie at the Skyline Theatre. Alton asked one of the girls if he could drive her home. I moved over to let her in. She was upset because she thought I was Alton's date. He had always said I was his 'baby sister.' He later married that girl, Laurel Harrow, December 19, 1954.

The folks decided that they were moving to Pueblo to be closer to Daddy's work. I stayed in Canon for a while with Gay than with Grandma Shaw until they found a place to live.

Mama, Daddy, and Alton lived for a short time northeast of Pueblo in an apartment on 29th Street. Then they moved into an old mining house, which had been relocated to Lewis Street west of Pueblo. It was a four-room house with no indoor plumbing, which they remodeled by building a kitchen, bathroom, and a small bedroom. I rejoined the family in the middle of the school year. I was very disappointed when I discovered the ninth was in Freed Junior high School.

I graduated from Centennial High School. I laid the tickets for the ceremony on top of the piano. Grandma Shaw was living with us then. Not realizing what they were she threw them away.

ARLENE JANOSKI

My father, Clarence Thomas Rapier died Jan. 9, 1979 in Pueblo, Colorado.

THE HEART THROBS OF MANY FATHERS AND MOTHERS
Oh. Father, help me understand,
And know the reason why.
The boy I loved did'st given me,
So early had to die;

The Answer
Grieve not, my son, for thine shall be
When death shall be no more.

unknown

I married when I turned eighteen. Mrsl Shultz, the girl's counselor, persuaded me to finish high school. I graduated in 1957 from Centennial High School in Pueblo, Colorado. I did not go to the Commencement as my Grandmother (Shaw) lived with us. Grandma was dusting the piano and accidentally threw the tickets away for the Commencement.

I am losing my family one by one:

My sister, Carol died Dec, 3, 2000. Services were held Dec. 9, at Grant Mortuary in Craig, Colorado.
My grandson, Buddy, died December 27, 1995.
My brother, Eugene, died March 1, 2004. March 5th he was buried in his temple cholthes at Utah Veterans Mamorial Park Cemetery.
Josephine died Octpber 22, 2005 is buried in Elkland, Missouri
Theodosia died Febuary 25, 2012 and is buried near Ogden, Utah.
My husband, Ray, died Janruary 4, 2019.

A MEMOIR OF THE RAPIER'S

Argul, Eugene and Carol back row.
Theodosia, Gay, Josephine and Alton front row
I am the baby.

The poem below was in a bible given to their mother, by Josephine and Theodosia, December 25, 1945.

> Has anyone seen three children or four
> Playing around my kitchen door?
> It was only a day or two ago—
> It can't be thirty years, I know—
> Since they tumbled and laughed in glee
> There in the shade of the old cherry tree.
> And I stood in the door and sighed
> When I thought of the clothes to be washed and dried.

Mrs. G. A. Cloyd

www.ingramcontent.com/pod-product-compliance
Lightning Source LLC
Chambersburg PA
CBHW021109080526
44587CB00010B/445